Worldly W[...]

Religions Enter Their Ecological Phase

MARY EVELYN TUCKER

With a Commentary by
Judith A. Berling

*Followed by a Response, Discussion,
and Epilogue*

The Second Master Hsüan Hua
Memorial Lecture

OPEN COURT
Chicago and La Salle, Illinois

To order books from Open Court, call 1-800-815-2280.
Visit our website at www.opencourtbooks.com.

Open Court Publishing Company is a division of Carus Publishing Company.

First printing 2003

Printed and bound in the United States of America.

Library of Congress Cataloging-in-Publication Data

Tucker, Mary Evelyn.
    Worldly wonder : religions enter their ecological phase / Mary Evelyn Tucker ; with a commentary by Judith A. Berling.
        p. cm. -- (The second Master Hsüan Hua memorial lecture)
    Includes bibliographical references and index.
    ISBN 0-8126-9529-1 (pbk. : alk. paper)
    1. Nature--Religious aspects. 2. Human ecology--Religious aspects.
I. Title. II. Master Hsüan Hua memorial lecture ; 2.
BL65.N35 T83 2003
291.2'4--dc21

                                                          2002156308

This book includes the text of a lecture sponsored by the Institute for World Religions and the Pacific School of Religion at Berkeley, California.

Worldly Wonder

CONTENTS

THE SECOND HSÜAN HUA
MEMORIAL LECTURE

*T*he Institute for World Religions, in partnership with the Pacific School of Religion and the Graduate Theological Union, sponsored the second annual Venerable Hsüan Hua Memorial Lecture in March 2002, in the Memorial Chapel of the Pacific School of Religion, Berkeley, California. The lecture series focuses on bringing the ancient wisdom of Asian religions and philosophy to bear on the pressing issues of the modern world, especially in the area of ethics and spiritual values.

The second Hsüan Hua Memorial Lecture was given by Mary Evelyn Tucker, professor of religion at Bucknell University in Lewisburg, Pennsylvania. Dr. Tucker teaches courses in world religions, Asian religions, and religion and ecology. She received her Ph.D. from Columbia University in the history of religions, specializing in Confucianism in Japan. She is the author of *Moral and Spiritual Cultivation in Japanese Neo-Confucianism* (1989), and has co-edited a series of works on ecology and religion, including

Worldviews and Ecology (1994), with John Grim; *Buddhism and Ecology* (1998), with Duncan Williams; *Confucianism and Ecology: The Interrelation of Heaven, Earth, and Humans* (1998), with John Berthrong; and *Hinduism and Ecology* (2000), with Christopher Key Chapple. She and John Grim directed a series of twelve conferences, "Religions of the World and Ecology," at Harvard's Center for the Study of World Religions. During the 2001–2002 academic year she was visiting professor at the Graduate Theological Union in Berkeley.

A lively response and discussion followed Professor Tucker's lecture. The discussion was preceded by a formal response given by Judith A. Berling, who is Professor of Chinese and Comparative Religion, a core doctoral faculty member, and a former dean and vice president for academic affairs at the Graduate Theological Union. Professor Berling earned her doctoral degree from Columbia University. Among her research interests are world religions and theological education, globalization, and Chinese spirituality. Her recent publications include "Taoism in Ming Culture" in *The Cambridge History of China*, Volume 8 (1998) and *A Pilgrim in Chinese Culture: Negotiating Religious Diversity* (1997). Dr. Berling's response, together with a transcript of questions from the audience and Dr. Tucker's replies, follow the text of Dr. Tucker's lecture in the present volume.

A BRIEF PORTRAIT
OF THE VENERABLE MASTER
HSÜAN HUA

"*I* have had many names," he once said, "and all
of them are false." In his youth in Manchuria, he was
known as "the Filial Son Bai"; as a young monk he
was An Tzu ("Peace and Kindness"); later, in Hong
Kong, he was Tu Lun ("Wheel of Rescue"); finally,
in America, he was Hsüan Hua, which might be
translated as "one who proclaims the principles of
transformation." To his thousands of disciples across
the world, he was always also "Shifu" —"Teacher."

Born in 1918 into a peasant family in a small
village on the Manchurian plain, Master Hua was the
youngest of ten children. He attended school for only
two years, during which he studied the Chinese
classics and committed many of them to memory.
As a young teenager, he opened a free school for both
children and adults. He also began then one of his
lifelong spiritual practices: reverential bowing.
Outdoors, in all weather, he would make over 800
prostrations daily, as a profound gesture of his respect
for all that is good and sacred in the universe.

He was nineteen when his mother died, and for three years he honored her memory by sitting in meditation in a hut beside her grave. It was during this time that he made a resolve to go to America to teach the principles of wisdom. As a first step, at the end of the period of mourning, he entered San Yuan Monastery, took as his teacher Master Chang Chih, and subsequently received the full ordination of a Buddhist monk at Pu To Mountain. For ten years he devoted himself to study of the Buddhist scriptural tradition and to mastery of both the Esoteric and the Ch'an Schools of Chinese Buddhism. He had also read and contemplated the scriptures of Christianity, Daoism, and Islam. Thus, by the age of thirty, he had already established through his own experience the four major imperatives of his later ministry in America: the primacy of the monastic tradition; the duty to educate; the need for Buddhists to ground themselves in traditional spiritual practice and authentic scripture; and, just as essential, the importance and the power of ecumenical respect and understanding.

In 1948, Master Hua traveled south to meet the Venerable Hsu Yun, who was then already 108 years old and China's most distinguished spiritual teacher. From him Master Hua received the patriarchal transmission in the Wei Yang Lineage of the Ch'an School. Master Hua subsequently left China for Hong Kong. He spent a dozen years there, first in seclusion, then later as a teacher at three monasteries that he founded.

Finally, in 1962, several of his Hong Kong disciples invited him to come to San Francisco. By 1968, Master Hua had established the Buddhist Lecture Hall in a loft in San Francisco's Chinatown, and there he began giving nightly lectures, in Chinese, to an audience of young Americans. His texts were the major scriptures of the Mahayana. In 1969, he astonished the monastic community of Taiwan by sending there, for final ordination, two American women and three American men, all five of them fully trained as novices, fluent in Chinese, and conversant with Buddhist scripture. During subsequent years, the Master trained and oversaw the ordination of hundreds of monks and nuns who came to California to study with him from all over North America, as well as from Europe, Australia, and Asia. These monastic disciples now teach in the twenty-eight temples, monasteries, and convents that the Master founded in the United States, Canada, and several Asian countries. The City of Ten Thousand Buddhas, located in California's North Coast 100 miles north of San Francisco, is home to over two hundred Buddhist monks and nuns, making it the largest Buddhist monastic community in North America.

Although he understood English well and spoke it when it was necessary, Master Hua almost always lectured in Chinese. His aim was to encourage Westerners to learn Chinese, so that they could become translators, not merely of his lectures, but of the major scriptural texts of the Buddhist Mahayana. His intent was realized. So far, the Buddhist Text Translation Society, which he founded, has issued over

130 volumes of translation of the major Sutras, together with a similar number of commentaries, instructions, and stories from the Master's teaching.

As an educator, Master Hua was tireless. From 1968 to the mid-1980s he gave as many as a dozen lectures a week, and he traveled extensively on speaking tours. He also established formal training programs for monastics and for laity; elementary and secondary schools for boys and for girls; Dharma Realm Buddhist University at the City of Ten Thousand Buddhas; and the Institute for World Religions, in Berkeley.

Throughout his life the Master taught that the basis of spiritual practice is moral practice. Of his monastic disciples he required strict purity, and he encouraged his lay disciples to adhere to the five precepts of the Buddhist laity. Especially in his later years, Confucian texts were often the subject of his lectures, and he held to the Confucian teaching that the first business of education is moral education. He identified six rules of conduct as the basis of communal life at the City of Ten Thousand Buddhas; the six rules prohibited contention, covetousness, self-seeking, selfishness, profiting at the expense of the community, and false speech. He asked that schoolchildren at the City recite these prohibitions every morning before class. In general, although he admired the independent-mindedness of Westerners, he believed that they lacked ethical balance and needed that stabilizing sense of public morality which is characteristic of the East.

The Venerable Master insisted on ecumenical respect, and he delighted in interfaith dialogue. He stressed commonalities in religious traditions—above all their emphasis on proper conduct, on compassion, and on wisdom. He was also a pioneer in building bridges between different Buddhist national traditions; for example, he often brought monks from Theravada countries to California to share the duties of transmitting the precepts of ordination. He invited Catholic priests to celebrate the mass in the Buddha Hall at the City of Ten Thousand Buddhas, and he developed a late-in-life friendship with Paul Cardinal Yu-Bin, the exiled leader of the Catholic Church in China and Taiwan. He once told Cardinal Yu-Bin: "You can be a Buddhist among the Catholics, and I'll be a Catholic among Buddhists." To the Master, the essential teachings of all religions could be summed up in a single word: wisdom.

ACKNOWLEDGMENTS

*F*or their thoughtful input to earlier versions of this manuscript I would like to extend special thanks to John Grim, Brian Swimme, Henry Rosemont, Diane Dumanoski, Gary Holthaus, Nancy Wright, Kusumita Pederson, Arthur Fabel, David Haberman, John Surrette, Marion Grau, and Whitney Bauman. I am indebted to Judith Berling for her insightful response. Gratitude too goes to the faculty of the Institute for World Religions for the invitation to deliver the second annual Venerable Master Hsüan Hua Memorial Lecture at the Pacific School of Religion in Berkeley, California. I send particular appreciation to Snjezana Akpinar for arranging the lecture, to David Rounds for editing the manuscript that appeared in *Religion East and West* and to Martin Verhoeven and David Ramsay Steele for bringing the book into its final published form.

There are those who have supported this process of birthing a new field in religion and ecology in special ways. They include Thomas Berry for his inspiring view of human-Earth relations, Martin Kaplan for his unflagging encouragement of the Harvard conference series and the Forum on Religion and Ecology, and the Kann Rasmussen, Germeshausen, and Winslow Foundations for their continued support. Tu Weiming, Michael McElroy, Anne Custer, Judith Korch, Laura Epperson, and Larry Sullivan have made possible the work at Harvard. I am grateful also to Bucknell University and especially to my department for time away from teaching. Stephanie Snyder in particular was unstinting in her help with many parts of this project.

It is to my parents that I dedicate this book for it is they who first showed me the myriad aspects of worldly wonder in both nature and in culture.

ACKNOWLEDGMENTS

Worldly Wonder

The Cosmological Context:
Evolution and Extinction

As we survey our human prospects on the threshold of this new millennium, we find our global situation fraught with particular irony. Over the past century, science has begun to weave together the story of a historical cosmos that emerged some thirteen billion years ago. The magnitude of this universe story is beginning to dawn on humans as we awaken to a new realization of the vastness and complexity of this unfolding process.[1] At the same time that this story becomes available to the human community, we are becoming conscious of the growing environmental crisis and of the rapid destruction of species and habitat that is taking place around the globe.[2] Just as we are realizing the vast expanse of time that distinguishes the evolution of the universe over some thirteen billion years, we are recognizing how late is our arrival in this stupendous process.[3] Just as we become conscious that the Earth took more than four billion years to bring forth this abundance of life, it is dawning on us how quickly we are foreshortening its future flourishing.

We need, then, to step back to assimilate our cosmological context. If scientific cosmology gives us an understanding of the origins and unfolding of the universe, the story of cosmology gives us a sense of our place in the universe. And if we are so radically affecting the story by extinguishing other life forms and destroying our own nest, what does this imply about our religious sensibilities or our sense of the sacred? As science is revealing to us the particular intricacy of the web of life, we realize we are unraveling it, although unwittingly in part. As we begin to glimpse how deeply embedded we are in complex ecosystems and dependent on other life forms, we see we are destroying the very basis of our continuity as a species. As biology demonstrates a fuller picture of the unfolding of diverse species in evolution and the distinctive niche of species in ecosystems, we are questioning our own niche in the evolutionary process. As the size and scale of the environmental crisis is more widely grasped, we are seeing our own connection to this destruction. We have become a planetary presence that is not always benign. We have become a religious presence that has atrophied.

This simultaneous bifocal recognition of our cosmological context and our environmental crisis is clearly demonstrated at the American Museum of Natural History in New York with two major new exhibits. One is the Rose Center that houses the Hall of the Universe and the Hall of the Earth. The other exhibit is the Hall of Biodiversity.

The Hall of the Universe is architecturally striking. It is housed in a monumental glass cube, in the center of which is a globe containing the planetarium. Suspended in space around the globe are the planets of our solar system. In a fascinating mingling of inner and outer worlds, our solar system is juxtaposed against the garden plaza and street scenes of New York visible through the soaring glass panels of the cube. After first passing through a simulation of the originating fireball, visitors move on to an elevated spiral pathway from which they participate in the exhibit. The sweeping pathway ushers the visitor into a descending walk through time that traces the thirteen-billion-year-old cosmic journey from the great flaring forth in the fireball, through the formation of galaxies, and finally to the emergence of our solar system and planet. It ends with the evolution of life in the Cenozoic period of the last sixty million years and concludes with one human hair under a circle of glass, with the hairsbreadth representing all of human history. The dramatic effect is stunning as we are called to re-image the human in the midst of such unfathomable immensities.

The Hall of Earth continues this evocation of wonder as it reveals the remarkable processes of the birth of the Earth, the evolution of the supercontinent, Pangaea, the formation of the individual continents, and the eventual emergence of life. It demonstrates the intricacy of plate tectonics, which was not widely accepted even as late as fifty years ago, and it displays geothermal life forms around deep-sea vents, which were only discovered a decade ago. This exhibit, then, illustrates how new our knowledge of the evolution of the Earth is and how much has been discovered within the last century.

In contrast to the vast scope of evolutionary processes evident in the Hall of the Universe and the Hall of the Earth, the Hall of Biodiversity displays the extraordinary range of life forms that the planet has birthed. A panoply of animals, fish, birds, reptiles, and insects engages the visitor. A plaque in the exhibit observes that we are now living in the midst of a sixth extinction period due to the current massive loss of species.[4] It notes that while the five earlier periods of extinction were caused by a variety of factors, including meteor collisions and climate change, humans are the primary cause of this present extinction spasm.[5]

With this realization, not only does our role as a species come into question, but our viability as a species remains in doubt. Along with those who recognized the enormity of the explosion of the atomic bombs in Japan, we are the first generations of humans to actually imagine our own destruction as a species.[6] And, while this may be extreme, some pessimists are suggesting this may not be such a regrettable event if other life forms are to survive.

The exhibition notes, however, that we can stem this tide of loss of species and habitat. The visitor walks through an arresting series of pictures and statistics where current destruction is recorded on one side and restoration processes are highlighted on the other. The contrasting displays suggest the choice is ours—to become a healing or a deleterious presence on the planet.

These powerful exhibits on cosmic evolution and on species extinction illustrate how science is helping us to enter into a macrophase understanding of the universe and of ourselves as a species among other species on a finite planet. The fact that the Rose Center is presenting the evolution of the universe and the Earth as an unfolding story in which humans participate is striking in itself. Indeed, the original introductory video to the Hall of the Universe observed that we are "citizens of the universe" born out of stardust and the evolution of galaxies, and that we are now responsible for its continuity. In addition, the fact that the Hall of Biodiversity suggests that humans can assist in stemming the current extinction spasm is a bold step for an "objective" and "unbiased" science-based museum. Scientists are no longer standing apart from what they are studying. They are assisting us in witnessing the ineffable beauty and complexity of life and its emergence over billions of years. This macrophase dimension of science involves three intersecting phases: understanding the story of the universe, telling the story as a whole, and reflecting on the story with a sense of our responsibility for its continuity.

The world's religions and scholars of those religions are also being called to contribute to this macrophase understanding of the universe story. The challenge for religions is both to revision our role as citizens of the universe and to reinvent our niche as members of the Earth community. This requires addressing such

cosmological questions as where we have come from
and where we are going. In other words, it necessitates
rethinking our role as humans within the larger
context of universe evolution as well as in the closer
context of natural processes of life on Earth. What
is humankind in relation to thirteen billion years of
universe history? What is our place in the framework
of 4.6 billion years of Earth history? How can we foster
the stability and integrity of life processes? These are
critical questions motivating the religion and ecology
dialogue.[7]

We might rephrase these questions in specifically
religious terms. Can religions situate their stories
within the universe story? Can they revision human
history within Earth history? Can the religions open
up their traditions to embrace the planet as home and
hearth? Can religions re-evoke and encourage the deep
sense of wonder that ignites the human imagination
in the face of nature's beauty?

For if the Earth is not in some sense a numinous
revelation of mystery, where indeed will the human
find mystery? And if humans destroy this awesome
matrix of mystery, where will we find sources of
inspiration pointing us toward the unfathomable
vastness of the sacred? Will religions assume a
disengaged pose as species go extinct, forests are
exterminated, soil, air, and water are polluted beyond
restoration, and human health and well-being
deteriorate? Or will they emerge from their concerns
with dogmas and policy regarding their own survival to

see that the survival of the myriad modes of life on Earth is also at stake?

We seek signs of hope, as we are poised at this simultaneous juncture of awakening to the wonder of cosmic evolution and of despairing at witnessing environmental destruction. Although our deleterious role as humans is becoming clearer, so, too, are various efforts emerging to mitigate the loss of species, restore ecosystems, prevent pollution of air, water, and soil, and preserve natural resources for future generations. The question for religious traditions, then, is how can they assist these processes and encourage humans to become a healing presence on the planet. Can religious traditions help us to find our niche as a species that does not overextend our effects and overshoot the limitations of fragile ecosystems?[8]

Indeed, the environmental crisis calls the religions of the world to respond by finding their voice within the larger Earth community. In so doing, the religions are now entering their ecological phase and finding their planetary expression.[9] They are awakening to a renewed appreciation of matter as a vessel for the sacred. Just as they have been working in the twentieth century to embrace diversity within the human community, so now they are called to encompass the diversity of life in the Earth community. From a concentration on God-human relations and human-human relations, they are being invited to reconfigure human-Earth relations. In Christianity, for example, human-Earth concerns have largely been framed in terms of Creator-Creation interaction. Christians are now called to reconstruct this configuration in terms of evolution and extinction.[10] From a concern for an ethics responding to the tragedies of homicide, suicide, and genocide, the world religions are being summoned to develop an ethics responding to biocide and geocide.[11] This expansion of concern is an invitation to extend comprehensive care and compassion toward the great fecundity of life that the planet has brought forth. It implies a decentering of the human and recentering of our lives within, not apart from, the myriad species with whom we share the planet. Their birthright becomes linked to ours; their flourishing is inseparable from ours; their continuity is intrinsically linked to ours.

The emergence, then, of the world's religions into their ecological phase and their planetary expression implies not simply reformation but transformation. For as they identify their resources for deeper ecological awakening—scriptural, symbolic, ritual, and ethical—they will be transforming the deep wellsprings of their tradition into a fuller expression. As they adapt their traditional resources and adopt new resources, they are creating viable modes of religious life beneficial not simply for humans but for the whole Earth community. This involves initiating and implementing new forms of the great wisdom traditions in a postmodern context and may involve opposition to certain aspects of modernity (such as relentless consumption) and change in other aspects of modernity (such as emphasizing individual rights, especially property rights, over communal responsibilities).

The great transformation of the religious traditions to their ecological phase calls forth enormous creativity of individuals and communities. It activates the human imagination toward a celebration of the awe and wonder of life—its emergence in the primal fireball, its unfolding in the universe story, and its flourishing in Earth's evolution. At the same time, this great transformation dynamizes human energy toward fulfilling the human role as a truly planetary species. It draws us into alignment with the Earth community. It invites us to participate in the flourishing of life on the planet; it evokes our celebration of worldly wonder.

This perspective calls us into contemplation of our own evolution as a planetary species with allegiance beyond regional or national boundaries. The inseparability of local and global—of hearth and cosmos—is breaking into human consciousness in myriad ways.[12] As part of the unfolding universe story, we celebrate our kinship not only with other humans but also with all life forms. We begin to find our niche. We realize we are not only part of humankind but of Earthkind; we are not simply human beings but universe beings. As such we are distinguished not merely by reflective consciousness but by wondering intelligence as well. This may be the indispensable capacity of humans that religions can evoke in the presence of the mystery of life. Along with gratitude, and reverence, wonder may be a key to release the flourishing potential of our species and our planet.

The Historical Context: Change and Continuity

THE QUESTION FOR THE WORLD'S RELIGIONS THEN (and for the scholars and theologians of those religions) is how can they answer this call to move toward their planetary expression in response to the magnitude of the environmental crisis. The world's religions, while grounded in foundational beliefs and practices, have never been static, but have always both effected change and been affected by change in response to intellectual, political, cultural, social, and economic forces. In light of this, they may, in fact, more accurately be described as religious processes rather than simply as preservers of traditions. As religious processes they have embraced change and transformation; as preservers of traditions they have embraced the security and continuity of the past. Both change and continuity have been present in the unfolding of religions, and this can be a source of their creative expression now, in response to the environmental crisis.

At the risk of oversimplifying complex historical lineages, one might suggest that there have been three major stages of the world's religions associated with civilizational developments: classical, medieval, and modern. The first is the classical era of the emergence of the major world religions and philosophy in the first Axial Age in the sixth century before the Common Era.[13] This is a period of remarkable flourishing of creative spiritual leaders, ranging from Confucius and Lao Tzu in East Asia, to Buddha and the Upanishadic seers in South Asia, to the Hebrew prophets of West Asia, and the pre-Socratic philosophers in Greece. The second stage is their medieval period of new syntheses that were often the result of dialogue with other religious or philosophical traditions. Examples are the recovery of the Aristotelian philosophical tradition by the medieval Christian scholastics, such as Thomas Aquinas, or the rise of Neo-Confucianism in China and the synthesis of Zhu Xi, partly in response to Buddhism and Daoism. The third stage is the modern period of the last five hundred years, following the age of encounter and the emergence of the Enlightenment in the West. In each of these eras, the religious traditions developed significant new schools of thought and practice in response to challenges from within as well as to pressures from without.

Some scholars of religion would describe our current situation as a fourth period characterized as "postmodernism." In our postmodern era, new constructive syntheses are emerging in light of deconstructive analyses of hegemonic thought along with liberating calls to move beyond outdated practices. Moreover, other scholars, such as Thomas Berry and Ewert Cousins, have observed that we are now in a second Axial period characterized by the global encounter of the world's religions. The first position calls for renewal within traditions, while the second calls for openness across traditions. We will discuss our postmodern circumstances when we highlight the limitations of religions in ecological dialogue and we will discuss the contemporary encounter of religions when we focus on inter-religious dialogue.

Our thesis here is that this fourth period may also be seen as a moment when religions are beginning to move into their ecological phase and find their planetary expression. From changes within religious communities and across religious communities, we are moving outward toward changes within the human-Earth community. To underscore the significance of these transformations, we will briefly highlight some of the intellectual currents of the third phase of modernity that have helped to shape our contemporary postmodern worldviews. These currents have emerged in the West and have now spread throughout the globe.

Among these complex tributaries to modernity are the humanist revolution that began in the fourteenth-century Renaissance, the expansionist revolution launched in the fifteenth-century age of exploration, the religious revolution of the sixteenth-century Reformation, the scientific revolution of the seventeenth century, the political revolution of the eighteenth-century Enlightenment, the economic revolution of nineteenth-century industrialization, the social revolution of twentieth-century human rights, and what we may call the ongoing ecological revolution of twentieth- and twenty-first-century environmental movements.

None of these are singular as revolutions; rather, they themselves are the results of myriad forces with multiple outcomes that have shaped modernity. The intersection of various currents of modernity with religious traditions has created significant challenges for religions. Renaissance humanism, for example, began the process of recentering the human body, mind, and spirit in a new configuration of import and meaning which celebrated the human over the divine. The age of exploration initiated the comprehensive interchange of culture, ideas, and goods that has opened religions to other cultures and religions, sometimes with deleterious consequences for the non-Western traditions. The Reformation initiated a major challenge to the dominance of the Roman Catholic Church, to its orthodox teachings, and to the role of individuals in interpreting scripture and seeking personal salvation. Since the rise of the Enlightenment in the West and the foregrounding of ideals of liberty, equality, and fraternity, new notions of reason, individualism, and freedom have emerged along with fresh concepts of social contract, the role of law, and the desirability of democratic processes. The Enlightenment has helped to shape the contours of secular humanism that have dominated significant aspects of our modern and postmodern world.

This was intensified with the scientific revolution of the seventeenth century, when religious cosmologies were severely called into question. The separation of reason and faith that began in the medieval period became more pronounced, and was further exacerbated by the emergence in the nineteenth century of the Darwinian theory of evolution, which religions are still trying to absorb. The human rights revolution of the twentieth century, which arose out of two world wars and the postcolonial era, has birthed a renewed sense of the dignity of the individual regardless of race, gender, ethnicity, or sexual preference. However, it has not yet sufficiently situated these individual human rights in relation to community responsibilities to other persons, other species, or the planet as a whole. As the industrial revolution of the nineteenth century coupled with market capitalism of the twentieth century spreads to every corner of the globe, religions are severely challenged to offer an alternative vision to the prevailing economic view of humans as primarily producers and consumers in the global market. Now the questions of the sustainability of life on the planet and the viability of our species give rise to a certain urgency in the ecological revolution and to new creative religious responses.

The particular modes of Western modernity which champion individualism, democracy, science, rationalism, and capitalism have now spread to Asia, Africa, and Latin America. From these encounters

across cultures, new forms of modernization—
economic, political, social—have emerged in the non-
Western world as well. At the same time, there are
significant contemporary movements around the globe
calling for constructive postmodern and postcolonial
perspectives. These movements tend to recognize the
limits of modernity in terms of reductionist science,
rational positivism, utilitarian economics, inflated
individualism, and exploitative politics.[14] It is here
that the emerging alliance of religion and ecology
might be fruitfully situated.[15] While drawing on
constructive aspects of modernity such as democratic
participation and the rich ethical resources of their
own traditions, the religions can stand in opposition
to the mindlessness of modernization processes which
threaten to destroy ecosystems and abuse natural
resources in the rush toward globalization.

Many theologians and religious leaders have
already spoken out against these modernization
processes, identifying them as part of an octopus-
like "economism" in the service of destructive
globalization.[16] They are forming alliances with
those who are alarmed by the unlimited economic
growth, rampant consumption, and overuse of natural
resources that are devouring the planet. They recognize
that these alluring economic pursuits are siphoning
off the enormous spiritual energies and creative
impulses of the human. The search for meaning has
become manipulated into materialist goals in the first
world and diverted into economic development at any

cost in the third world. The natural and human worlds suffer as both the environment and human communities deteriorate in the race toward unrestrained economic globalization. Even the call for sustainability has frequently been manipulated by the drive for profit and growth rather than restraint. The alternative voices of the religions are needed, then, to imagine and create other possibilities for human life besides the accumulation and consumption that undermine fragile ecosystems and deplete natural resources. Surely religions in their postmodern phase can inspire larger aspirations for our place and purpose in nature than simply economic exploitation. The question arises: is the Earth a commodity to be bought and sold or a community of life that invites participation?

The Religious Context: Problems and Promise

THE SCOPE AND COMPLEXITY of the environmental crisis as situated within the varied intellectual, political, social, or economic revolutions of the last several centuries present significant challenges to the world's religions as they emerge into their ecological phase. A primary challenge involves acknowledging the limitations of religious traditions as well as underscoring their potential and actual contributions. This section will identify some of the limitations or problems of religions in responding adequately to the environmental crisis as well as the contributions and promise of the religions in their emerging dialogue with ecological issues.

In acknowledging their problematic dimensions, we need to underscore the dark side of religious traditions as well as their lateness in awakening to the environmental crisis. In addition, we should note the ever-present gap between ideal principles and real practices as well as the inevitable disjunction between modern environmental problems and traditional religious resources. For all of these reasons, religions are necessary but not sufficient for solutions to environmental problems. Thus they need to be in dialogue with other religions and other disciplines in focusing on environmental issues.

We must begin, then, with both humility and boldness as we note the obstacles and opportunities confronting religious traditions in this emerging dialogue of religion and ecology. We note first the dark side of religions. The human energy poured into religious traditions can clearly be unleashed in both violent and compassionate ways as has been demonstrated throughout history, especially recent history. While the causes of conflict and war are frequently economic, political and environmental, the religious dimensions need to be understood as well. Even before the September 11th terrorist attacks, the near genocide against Native Americans on this continent and against Jews in Europe would be sufficient manifestations of this. In addition, the numerous religious wars that arose in Western Europe and currently the religious conflicts in the Balkans, the Middle East, and South Asia are further evidence of the destructive dimensions of religious convictions, especially in service to exclusive claims to truth.

It is important to acknowledge also that religions are only one factor among many others contributing to new patterns of human-Earth relations promoting the flourishing of life. Religions can be isolated from critical contemporary issues and estranged from other institutions or disciplines involved in social and ecological change. For example, religions are sometimes antagonistic to science, both in assumptions and methods. Significant efforts have been made in the last several decades to assist in overcoming this antagonism.[17]

Religions have thus been late in coming to environmental discussions and they need to be in conversation with those individuals and groups who have been working on environmental issues for many decades.[18] While there is growing evidence of the vitality of the emerging dialogue of religion and ecology, and while there are remarkable examples around the world of grassroots environmental action inspired by religion, it is clear that environmental changes will come from many different disciplines, motivations, and inspirations.

With these qualifications in mind, we recognize nonetheless that religions historically have been forces for positive change, liberating human energy for efficacious personal, social, and political transformation. This potential for identifying resources for positive transformation is helping to shape the dialogue of religion and ecology.

It was in this spirit of recognizing both the problems and the promise of religions that an international conference series, entitled "Religions of the World and Ecology," was held at the Center for the Study of World Religions at Harvard. The series critically explored attitudes toward nature in the world's religious traditions and highlighted environmental projects around the world inspired by religious values. From 1996 to1998, a series of ten conferences examined the traditions of Judaism, Christianity, Islam, Hinduism, Jainism, Buddhism, Daoism, Confucianism, Shinto, and indigenous religions. The conferences, organized by John Grim and myself in collaboration with a team of area specialists, brought together international scholars of the world's religions as well as environmental activists and leaders. Recognizing that religions are key shapers of people's worldviews and formulators of their most cherished values, this broad research project has identified both ideas and practices supporting a sustainable environmental future. The papers from these conferences are being published in a series of ten volumes from the Center for the Study of World Religions and Harvard University Press.[19]

In the autumn of 1998, three culminating conferences were held at the American Academy of Arts and Sciences in Cambridge, Massachusetts, at the United Nations, and at the American Museum of Natural History in New York. These events brought representatives of the world's religions into conversation with one another as well as into dialogue with key scientists, economists, educators, and policy makers from various environmental fields. A multireligious and multidisciplinary approach was inaugurated.

A major result of these conferences was the establishment of an ongoing Forum on Religion and Ecology that was announced at a United Nations press conference to continue the research, education, and outreach begun at the earlier conferences. A primary goal of the Forum is to develop a field of study in religion and ecology that has implications for public policy. Toward this end the Forum has mounted a comprehensive website under the Harvard Center for the Environment (http://harvard.environment. edu/religion). It has sponsored workshops for high school teachers, and has organized various conferences at Harvard and on the west coast on World Religions and Animals; on Nature Writers and the Ecological Imagination; and on Cosmology in Science and Religion. The intention is to suggest the movement outward of cosmological awareness and ethical concerns from the human sphere to embrace other species, the larger web of the natural world, and the cosmos at large.

Just as religions played an important role in creating sociopolitical changes in the twentieth century through moral challenges for the extension of human rights, so now in the twenty-first century religions are contributing to the emergence of a broader cosmological orientation and environmental ethics based on diverse sensibilities regarding the sacred dimensions of the more-than-human world.[20] They are moving from a primarily anthropocentric focus to include ecocentric and cosmocentric concerns. This movement acknowledges that much work remains to be done in the human realm in relation to issues of social, economic, and political justice. Yet it is increasingly clear that social and environmental issues can no longer be seen as separate concerns. The religion-and-ecology field embraces this continuity in helping to create the grounds for long-term sustainable human-Earth relations.

In these efforts it is important to keep in mind that there is inevitably a gap between theory and practice, between ideas and action. This is perhaps one of the major obstacles to the efficacy of religion in environmental discussions. The expectations placed on religions are often unrealistically high because the desire for religions to be ideal models is so great. It is easy to point out inadequacies and thus dismiss the religious traditions as ineffective or hypocritical.

In identifying potential and actual ecological resources from the world's religions, it is important to recognize the complexity of the relationship of ideal and real at the outset and to avoid idealizing any one religion as having the best theories or practices. It will also be critical to examine the historical record of cultures and traditions, as environmental historians are beginning to do. Finally, we can observe that even as the ecological attitudes of religions begin to change we can ask: will practice follow of its own accord, or will religions have to be prodded to translate ideas into action?

In light of these qualifications we can cultivate an appropriate hermeneutics of suspicion regarding blanket claims to environmental purity in theory or in practice. For example, many have described Native American or other indigenous traditions as especially ecologically sensitive. However, not all indigenous practices can be defended as environmentally sound; one example is the slash and burn agriculture practiced by indigenous peoples in some parts of Southeast Asia. It is also frequently claimed that the traditions of Asia are more attuned to nature, especially Buddhism and Daoism. Rich ecological resources clearly reside in these traditions. Yet otherworldly movements toward withdrawal into individual meditation or the quest for personal liberation or immortality cast doubt on any such unqualified claims about these traditions. In truth, among the religious traditions, the record is mixed with regard to their ecologically friendly resources, both historically and at present. Moreover, ecologically relevant texts do not necessarily result in ecologically appropriate practices.

The Harvard conference series and the resulting volumes on world religions and ecology were designed to begin examining the multiple resources of the traditions both theoretically and practically. Further studies need to be done on these resources as well as on the actual historical records of the traditions in relation to environmental practices.

In this spirit, the emerging dialogue on religion and ecology also acknowledges that in seeking long-term environmental solutions, there is clearly a disjunction between contemporary problems regarding the environment and traditional religions as resources. The religious traditions are not equipped to supply specific guidance in dealing with complex issues such as climate change, desertification, or deforestation. At the same time certain orientations and values from the world's religions may not only be useful but even indispensable for a more comprehensive cosmological orientation and environmental ethics.[21]

The disjunction of traditional religious resources and modern environmental problems in their varied cultural contexts needs to be highlighted so that new conjunctions can be identified. We acknowledge that religious scriptures and commentaries were written in an earlier age with a different audience in mind. Similarly, many of the myths and rituals of the world's religions were developed in earlier historical contexts, frequently agricultural, while the art and symbols were created within worldviews very different from our own. Likewise, the ethics and morality of the world's religions respond primarily to anthropocentric perspectives regarding the importance of human-

human relations, and the soteriology and spirituality are formulated in relation to theological perspectives of enhancing divine-human relations.

Despite these historical and cultural contingencies, there are particular religious attitudes and practices as well as common ethical values that can be identified for broadening and deepening environmental perspectives. Thus we affirm the actual and potential contribution of religious ideas for informing and inspiring ecological theology, environmental ethics, and grass-roots activism. Religions are now reclaiming and reconstructing these powerful religious attitudes, practices, and values toward reconceiving mutually enhancing human-Earth relations. Careful methodological reflection is needed in considering how to bring forward in coherent and convincing ways the resources of religious traditions in response to particular aspects of our current environmental crisis. It entails a self-reflexive yet creative approach to retrieving and reclaiming texts and traditions, re-evaluating and re-examining what will be most efficacious, and thus restoring and reconstructing religious traditions in a creative postmodern world. All of this involves a major effort to evoke the power and potential of religious traditions to function even more effectively as sources of spiritual inspiration and moral transformation in the midst of the environmental challenges faced by the Earth community.

Pluralistic Perspectives: Multireligious and Multidisciplinary Approaches

No one religious tradition or discipline will be sufficient in the search for a more comprehensive and culturally inclusive global environmental ethics. Thus the multireligious dimensions of this effort need to be underscored. Dialogue between and among religious traditions around environmental concerns is already taking place. Similarly, a multidisciplinary approach to environmental problems is emerging in academia, in policy institutes, and in national and international agencies focusing on the environment. These discussions need to become more sophisticated and integrated. Such multireligious and mutidisciplinary discussions have emerged in various international arenas such as the Parliament of the World's Religions in Chicago in 1993 and in Capetown in 1999, the Tehran Seminar on Environment, Culture, and Religion held in Iran in June 2001, and the Earth Dialogues on "Globalization: Is Ethics the Missing Link?" held in Lyon, France, in February 2002.[22]

The world's religions are now international presences with followers well beyond the country or culture of origin. Their international presence is part of their enormous potential to effect change in attitudes toward the environment. Religions are flourishing around the world, even in China and Russia where

communism intended to stamp out the need for
religion, and despite the prediction that religions would
disappear as modernization arose and secularization
spread.[23] The international presence of religion means
multi-religious dialogue is more crucial than ever
before.

Pluralism thus needs to be highlighted and
celebrated, especially as we realize the extraordinary
migration patterns that have occurred around the globe
in the twentieth century. More than at any other time
in history, people have migrated from their homelands
due to adverse economic, political, and environmental
conditions. As the Pluralism Project at Harvard has so
comprehensively documented, the entire landscape
of American religious life has changed radically
since the doors of immigration were opened with the
Immigration Act of 1965. In addition, demographics
show that in several years Islam will be the largest
religion in the world. Already the majority of Muslims
live outside the Arab world. Likewise, the majority of
Christians are located in Asia, Africa, and Latin
America.

Tolerance and celebration of diversity are
essential as we try to create the conditions for a
sustainable future. Diversity is enormously valuable
in both human and biotic communities. Ecosystem
models tell us that the health of biotic communities
depends on diversity and exchange. So, too, the
health of the human community depends on diversity.
Just as monoculture farming is problematic for

ecosystems and for healthy agriculture, so can monoculture in human societies result in blandness and lack of creative exchange of ideas. This is especially true in religious communities. Historically and at present, religious traditions have grown and developed in creative interaction with other religions as well as in response to internal institutional and intellectual challenges. This has resulted in new syntheses within traditions and across traditions.

Failure to appreciate diversity has serious consequences, among them a religious triumphalism that highlights the virtues of one tradition as opposed to those of another. Similarly, the exclusivism of truth claims creates the potential for conflict and resentment and can give rise to rigid hegemonic or fundamentalist perspectives. While truth claims within religions need to be respected, different avenues to truth also need to be honored. Fortunately, in the last four decades, inter-religious dialogues have prepared the grounds for religious pluralism to be better understood. Indeed, these dialogues have moved from appreciation of differences to recognition of the urgent need for even greater cooperation for the sake of both the human and natural communities. Thus inter-religious dialogue has broadened its focus to include not only theological topics such as the nature of God and spiritual topics such as meditation and prayer but also shared ethical perspectives on social justice, human rights, and, more recently, the environment.[24]

Lasting ethical solutions to our global environmental and social problems will need to come from diverse perspectives. Here the world's religious traditions are a major resource. In addition, important work is being done within and outside of academia in environmental philosophy and in environmental and social ethics, drawing on science, philosophy, literature, and other sources. A broader ethical synthesis can emerge with such an exchange of ideas. Indeed, the search for a comprehensive global ethics has already benefited from the input of the world's religions in such documents as the "Earth Charter"[25] (See Appendix IV) and "Towards a Global Ethic: An Initial Declaration" issued at the Parliament of World Religions in 1993.

Religions, however, will need to be self-reflective and self-critical rather than self-promotional in contributing to environmental discussions, especially in international forums. When participants are attuned to both the special insights and the limitations of their particular traditions, a global ethics can indeed emerge. Examples may be seen in the current rethinking of issues such as population, development, and the role of women. Multireligious discussions are essential for identifying what will be helpful and what will be problematic in diverse religious perspectives. Lessons can be learned from the field of human rights, where religious and cultural diversity have been highlighted with beneficial results. For example, many scholars have identified minimum standards for universal human rights along with the recognition of the importance of cultural diversity.[26]

Thus, with the realization of the critical nature of the environmental crisis, multi-religious dialogue is being drawn into a search for both a common ground and common good beyond the particular differences and historical conflicts of the religions. The common ground is the Earth itself as an expression of numinous creativity, a matrix of mystery, and a locus for encountering the sacred. This common ground of mystery is in danger of being blindly wasted. It can be said, then, that the environmental crisis may disclose not only the common ground of the mystery of the Earth itself, but also the higher ground beyond differences in the search for the common good to promote the flourishing of life. In this effort common ground and common good are joined.

Just as multireligious perspectives are indispensable, so too multidisciplinary approaches to environmental problems are clearly needed.[27] It is, in fact, encouraging to note that entirely new multidisciplinary fields of environmental study and policy are already being established both within academia and without. Key examples of these are the push for limits to growth and new cost accounting coming from ecological economics, the emergence of the fields of conservation biology and restoration ecology within science, the movement toward ecological security and sustainability from the international political community, and the development of renewable energy, alternative technologies, ecological design, and biomimicry coming from many areas including architecture and engineering.

In the humanities, important multidisciplinary fields of study are emerging in environmental history, literature, and philosophy. Religion and ecology can be situated as a new field of study in the humanities that is similarly multidisciplinary in outlook and in concern. From the perspective of this field, based within religious studies or theology, the contributions of religions to environmental studies and policy may become clarified. This is particularly true as various religious and cultural attitudes toward nature are identified.

This emerging field of religion and ecology, then, looks both inward and outward. It looks inward to the resources of the traditions, historically and at present, that foster mutually beneficial human-Earth relations. At the same time it looks outward toward dialogue with those in other disciplines such as science, economics, and policy, knowing that lasting cultural changes will depend on such key intersections.

In addition to the practical skills and insights from various disciplines, multiple ethical motivations for environmental protection and restoration can be identified. This includes appreciation of the intrinsic value of nature and the critical importance of biodiversity, acknowledgement of aesthetic and recreational needs for contacts with nature, improvement of human health by protecting water, air, and soil, and the rights of future generations to a sustainable life.

Secular humanists and religious believers often share these motivations, especially the importance of valuing nature intrinsically.[28] This contrasts sharply with the predominantly utilitarian drives that tend to motivate business. Thus environmentalists usually feel that unrestricted economic development and the exploitative use of nonrenewable resources are problematic. For many environmentalists logging and road building should be limited in national forests, oil should not be extracted from pristine reserves or coastal regions, and the rights of spotted owls and other species to exist and to populate their own habitat should be honored. These views have sometimes led to acrimonious conflicts between environmentalists and those concerned with economic development. This is especially true in international conferences and discussions at the United Nations where third world countries sometimes want to push forward with development goals often at the expense of the environment. This was a source of tension at the United Nations Conference on Environment and Development (UNCED) at Rio de Janeiro in 1992, and at the United Nations World Summit on Sustainable Development (WSSD) in Johannesburg in 2002.

This tension is highlighted when one reflects on the fact that one billion people live on $1 per day and some two billion people exist on $2 per day. The ravages of poverty on people and the environment cannot go unaddressed. The lure of economic development is real for so many who long for minimum sources of food, clothing, shelter, and employment. Drinkable water and breathable air are becoming scarce commodities in many parts of the world. When one factors in the more than two billion people in India and China alone who seek a better standard of living for themselves and their children, one wonders how this can be managed without massive destruction of the life systems of the planet. The rapid deterioration of cities and countryside in South and East Asia in the last thirty years is a chilling reminder of the complex issues we face as a planetary species. Can we in the industrialized world deny the minimum fruits of modernization to the less-developed countries? How to manage this without exacerbating the already fractious relations between developed and developing countries is a major challenge. Yet there are before us many models of alternative technologies and energy sources, sustainable agriculture, green businesses, and environmental education that can be invoked for the transformations ahead. We need not destroy ourselves with unrestrained development that ultimately impoverishes both people and the planet.

Most environmentalists are wary of short-term projects for profit that do not take into account the long-term effects on species, habitat, and resources. Their anxiety arises from a variety of ethical motivations that include a concern for the immediate well-being of land and species as well as for the welfare of present and future generations. In attempting to reconcile these apparent conflicts between economics and ecology, broader intergenerational and interspecies environmental ethics are being developed that suggest human responsibilities should extend to future generations of all species. In addition, the call for the precautionary principle to be operative is becoming more widespread. This encourages the mindful prevention of pollution before it occurs. All of these are reasons why the Earth Charter is such a critical document.

In many of these sometimes heated discussions of economic development versus environmental protection, the world's religions can play a vital role. This is especially true in providing both spiritual resources and insights as well as culturally particular but globally comprehensive environmental ethics. Of particular relevance here are the common concerns of *reverence* for the Earth, *respect* for other species, *responsibility* to the welfare of future generations, *restraint* in the consumption of resources, and *redistribution* of goods and services more equitably. In summary, the contributions of religions are one part of a larger complex of various disciplines and motivations. Multidisciplinary approaches and the development of comprehensive environmental ethics will be indispensable for long-term environmental solutions. Religions are beginning to contribute to these endeavors.

The Transformative Context:
Reclaiming and Reconstructing

The challenge, then, for religions (and for scholars of religions) is how to participate in this transformative moment by reclaiming and reconstructing religious traditions so as to promote flourishing human-Earth relations. This will involve the careful retrieval of selected scriptures and commentaries, symbols and myths, rituals and prayers. It will also require the re-evaluation of particular beliefs and practices in light of the environmental crisis. Finally, it will necessitate the reconstruction of traditions in their fuller planetary expression.

This section will explore several key topics in this process of retrieving, re-evaluating, and reconstructing traditions, namely dogma, rituals and symbols, moral authority, soteriology, and ethics. Within these topics we will highlight some of the creative tensions that are involved in such reconstructive processes. These creative tensions are intended to be viewed as dyadic and interpenetrating relationships rather than as irreconcilable dualisms. In other words, our aim is to see such tensions as interrelated forces, not as clashing opposites. In the space between such creative tensions there can emerge the deeply motivating spiritual resources of the religious traditions toward grounded transformative action.

1 DOGMA: ORTHODOXY VERSUS DIALOGUE

As teachers of doctrinal truth or dogma, some individuals or institutions in particular traditions assume self-appointed roles as repositories of orthodoxy. These individuals or institutions tend to be conservative in that they wish to preserve particular versions of "truth," which they sometimes claim as special revelation through scripture. Consequently, religious traditions can promote triumphalism and exclusivity that may lead to proselytizing and even to violence. The counterpoint is that religions are constantly being brought into dialogue with contemporary issues and ideas, and thus they continue to change. Furthermore, as noted earlier, religions throughout their history have frequently been in active conversation with other religious traditions and been transformed in response to this dialogue. Indeed, the changes may be in the form of syncretism and fusion of religions, as is frequently the case in East Asia and South Asia. The major counterweight to rigid orthodoxy or exclusivist claims to truth is ecumenical and inter-religious dialogues.

During the last forty years, significant steps have been taken in ecumenical and inter-religious dialogues. The Christian churches have held important ecumenical meetings to discuss differences of doctrine. Moreover, significant inter-religious discussions have taken place between Christians and Jews, Christians and Buddhists, and Christians and Confucians. With

WORLDLY WONDER

regard, then, to ecological issues, the ground for further inter-religious discussion has already been prepared. There is thus great potential for focusing inter-religious dialogue on the urgency of the environmental crisis. With several decades of preparation, the religions may be poised to move beyond dogmatism to a shared sense of the common good of the planet. This may result in a renewal for the religious traditions themselves through a restoration of the planet.

Examples of such cooperation include international multi-religious projects such as the Forum on Religion and Ecology (FORE) based at Harvard; the Alliance of Religion and Conservation (ARC) based in England; and the World Faiths Development Dialogue (WFDD), also based in England. Within nations, important long-term efforts include the National Religious Partnership for the Environment (NRPE) in the United States and the Zimbabwean Institute of Religious Research and Ecological Conservation (ZIRRCON). Also, major international conferences involving the world's religious leaders and laity have focused on the environment. Among them are the Global Forum of Spiritual and Parliamentary Leaders in Oxford in 1988, in Moscow in 1990, in Rio de Janeiro in 1992, in Kyoto in 1993; the Parliament of World Religions in Chicago in 1993 and in Capetown in 1999; and the Millennium World Peace Summit of Religious and Spiritual Leaders at the United Nations in 2001.

2 RITUALS AND SYMBOLS: TRADITIONAL OR TRANSFORMATIVE

Religions are also inheritors of cultural traditions and as such they may become ritually constrained or fossilized in forms of worship. Ritual and prayer can become rote or remote while symbols and images may no longer convey the depth of meaning they originally embodied. As a result, rituals and symbols are reduced to flattened forms of reference. The connection to the living biological context in which they are embedded may need renewal or reactivation. For religious rituals and symbols to be vibrant, they need to be connected to the living world, even if they point beyond it. A deep numinous mystery resides in this connection and when rituals and symbols are disconnected from this reality they cannot activate a resonance with the ineffable power that sustains life. Hence, they become withered and attenuated.

The historian of religion, Mircea Eliade reminded us of this when he illuminated the implicit layering of references from the natural world underlying Christian rituals and symbols.[29] Central to Christianity is the reflection on birth, death, and rebirth that is present in the natural world. The liturgical cycle is set entirely within the larger rhythms of nature's seasons. Christmas is situated at the winter solstice with the return of light; Easter is celebrated at the spring equinox and the renewal of life. The sacraments, too, draw on the rich bounty of the natural world. The

Eucharist uses bread and wine associated with harvest, thanksgiving, and life-regenerating processes. Baptism uses water to welcome an individual into a community of faith. In monastic life the cycle of daily prayers is coordinated with the diurnal turning of the planet around the sun.

A contemporary example of opening traditional forms of ritual and symbol into their ecological phase is the *Missa Gaia* or Earth Mass with the music of Paul Winter. This moves the Christian Mass into its planetary expression. The Earth Mass has been celebrated for the last two decades in October on the feast of St. Francis of Assisi at the Cathedral of St. John the Divine in New York City. Many local parishes across the country have been inspired to hold similar rituals. Returning to recapture the spirit of Francis with regard to the animals and the inspiration of medieval cathedrals in fostering community, St. John's opens its great entry doors for the procession of the animals down the main aisle and the blessing of the animals in the context of the Earth Mass.

Other examples of contemporary ecological rituals can also be identified from among the world's religions. These include the Hindu ritual of tree planting as likened to a *prasad* offering in South India, the Theravada Buddhist monk's ordaining of trees in Thailand so as to stop loggers from clear-cutting the forest, Shona and Christian tree planting in Zimbabwe to counteract deforestation after the civil war, the Jewish practice of observing Shabbat to allow time for rest and rejuvenation of individuals and communities, and the Jain respect for life so that meat or fish are not eaten.[30]

Dialogue between religion and ecology can revivify rituals and symbols in light of the current environmental crisis. Moreover, it can assist in awakening a renewed appreciation for the intricate cosmological web of life in which we dwell.

3 MORAL AUTHORITY: OPPRESSIVE OR LIBERATING

As conservators of moral authority, religious traditions can become institutionally rigid citadels of power. The misuse of power by religions has been documented throughout history. It is all too familiar and need not be elaborated here. The authoritarian aspects of religion are often what make people flee its influence. Institutional moral authority, however, can be oppressive or liberating according to how it is invoked. Religions can be cradles of conformity or vessels of creativity. They can be suppressors of change or beacons of transformation.

The narrowness of religions can also be seen in the fact that most of them have been gender biased, some have been militantly ethnocentric, and others have been racially prejudiced. In the twentieth century, liberation movements for human rights have helped to overcome some of these constraints. Indeed, the religious traditions themselves have often provided leadership for these movements, recognizing the inherent dignity of the individual and the right to equitable employment, decent housing, and adequate education.

Discussions of human rights have broadened to include a sense not only of individuals but also of communities, both of the human and the more-than-human worlds. For example, feminist studies have expanded their focus to identify the degradation of women and the Earth as part of a continuity of the devaluation of matter. By the same token, these ecofeminist studies have suggested that attention to women's concerns and to the nurturing of the Earth need to be seen as part of a larger social transformation of consciousness, without essentializing women by identifying them exclusively with the Earth. Recent ecofeminist thinking in the world religions has helped to expand environmental discourse and pluralize its perspectives by foregrounding women of various ethnic and racial backgrounds.[31]

Similarly, by seeing environmental racism as morally problematic, religions have helped to expand the focus for human rights to include the right to a clean and healthy environment. This has involved identifying previously invisible arenas of racial prejudice and environmental injustice where minority communities have been viewed as dispensable and have been used as dumping grounds for waste, incineration, and pollution. Black, Hispanic, and Native American communities in the United States and African communities abroad have been particular victims of these callous attitudes whereby the excesses of industrial society have been deposited in their communities. Religious leadership has helped to uncover these problems and called for their rectification. The United Church of Christ statement on environmental justice is particularly important in this regard.

While much remains to be done, it can be said that Christian churches in the twentieth century have embraced teachings regarding social justice and human rights and brought them out of the words of encyclicals, pastoral letters, and policy statements and into the world with calls for racial and economic equity. (Gender equity still seems to lag behind, however.) For example, in the Jubilee 2000 movement, Christian churches urged the World Bank and major lending institutions to consider debt reduction for poor nations.[32] Religions have the potential for similar transformative leadership in the area of ecology, justice, and the future of life forms on the planet.[33]

No other group of institutions can wield the particular moral authority of the religions, notwithstanding the abuses this authority has also been subject to. Thus the efficacy of religions in encouraging individuals and communities to protect the environment is considerable in potentiality and demonstrable in actuality. Indeed, many scientists have recognized this. They have called upon the religious traditions to provide a compelling moral force for drawing citizens into a larger sense of concern for the reality of environmental degradation. The scientists note the potential of religions for highlighting the awe and wonder of nature and the need to preserve it for present and future generations of all species. Examples of this appear in key documents such as "Preserving and Cherishing the Earth: An Appeal for Joint Commitment in Science and Religion," released in 1990; "The Joint Appeal in Religion and Science: Statement by Religious Leaders at the Summit on Environment," published in 1991; "World Scientists' Warning to Humanity," issued by the Union of Concerned Scientists in 1992 (See Appendices I, II, and III). More recently, in the United States the Coalition on Environment and Jewish Life (COEJL) and the National Council of Churches have conducted campaigns on climate change. This has highlighted the moral authority of Jewish and Protestant leaders in relation to this massive global problem. Similarly, the "Common Declaration by Pope John Paul II and the Ecumenical Patriarch Bartholomew I" has had wide circulation. (See Appendix V)[34]

4   SOTERIOLOGY: WORLDLY OR OTHERWORLDLY?

In discussing the positive and negative dimensions of religions with regard to environmental issues it is sometimes observed that religions can tend toward an otherworldly soteriology. In other words, they have a salvific orientation that privileges the divine as residing in the transcendent world of Heaven, Nirvana, Moksha, or the Pure Land. This encourages concentration on personal salvation or liberation out of this world and into the next. The critical question arises: How, then, can religions be attentive to this world and to the environment? When the transcendent becomes primary, what happens to the sense of the divine or the immanent reality in nature? It should be noted, however, that indigenous traditions stand in stark contrast to this otherworldly orientation in their participation in natural cosmological processes.

It is undeniable that an otherworldly orientation and a focus on personal salvation in some of the world's religions can create a tendency to see this world as simply a vale of tears to be endured and ultimately transcended. The sometimes exclusive focus on an individual's relationship with God or the divine can diminish the sense of the importance of the Earth. Worship, prayer, and meditation are often directed at purifying the soul, praising God, or getting rid of ego in order to advance toward the goal of personal salvation. The consequence of this orientation toward the next world and personal salvation is the tendency in some religions to devalue nature and deny the importance or even the reality of matter. Redemption out of the world as fallen and liberation into a Heavenly realm is seen as a primary aim. This dualism that divides matter from spirit and privileges spirit as the highest good has created ambivalent attitudes toward nature in a number of the world's religions.[35]

That many religious traditions have elements of an other-worldly orientation is not necessarily an exclusive or defining concern. Religions can, in fact, embrace both world-affirming and world-negating dimensions. In Christianity, for example, the idea of the Kingdom of God may be used to establish criteria for justice on Earth or for entry into a paradisal world beyond. Similarly, in Mahayana Buddhism, the Pure Land is seen as a salvific next world, while the Tathagatagarbha doctrine affirms the Buddha Nature as present in the natural world. In Daoism, achieving immortality may be a long-term goal, but practices are encouraged that induce health in this life such as balanced diet, meditation and breathing, and movement exercises like *tai qi* and *qi gong*. These exercises place the practitioner in alignment with nature through drawing on the elements and on the varied movements of animals, insects, and birds.

Thus, it is helpful to recognize that there may be fruitful and creative tensions between the transcendent and immanent dimensions of the world's religions. In other words, the pull toward wholeness, completion, and fulfillment represented by the transcendent longings of the human can be balanced by a sense of reverence, reciprocity, and care for the fecundity of life that reflects the presence of the divine in this world. The here and hereafter can be seen in a creative dialectic of intimacy and distance, of commitment to change in the world along with detachment from the fruits of one's actions.[36] In Christianity, for example, the broadening of certain theological or sacramental perspectives may enhance an appreciation of the beauty and sacrality of this world without diminishing the sense of a larger reality beyond this world. Through a renewed sense of the incarnational dimensions of Christianity, there may emerge a more encompassing Christology that embraces the Cosmic Christ of the universe.[37] Similarly, a richer sacramental theology may be articulated which recognizes all of nature as part of a sacred reality. The work of Matthew Fox and others to identify a Creation-Centered Spirituality in the Christian tradition have been an important contribution to these efforts.[38]

5   ETHICS: ANTHROPOCENTRIC OR ANTHROPOCOSMIC

The focus of ethics in the world's religions has been largely human-centered. Humane treatment of humans is often seen not only as an end in itself but also as a means to eternal reward. While some have criticized this anthropocentric perspective of world religions as rather narrow in light of environmental degradation and the loss of species, it is nonetheless important to recall that this perspective has also helped to promote major movements for social justice and human rights.

While social justice is an ongoing and unfinished effort of engagement, the challenge for the religions is also to enlarge their ethical concerns to include the more than human world. Social justice and environmental integrity are now being seen as part of a continuum. For some decades environmental philosophers have been developing the field of environmental ethics that can now provide enormous resources for the world's religions in considering how to expand their ethical focus. Emerging biocentric, zoocentric, and ecocentric ethics are attentive to life forms, animal species, and ecosystems within a planetary context. A new "systems ethics" of part and whole, local and global, will assist the religions in articulating a more comprehensive form of environmental ethics from within their traditions. This is a major part of the development of religions into their ecological phase.

Thus religions can move from exclusively anthropocentric ethics to ecocentric ethics and even to anthropocosmic ethics. The latter is a term used by Tu Weiming to describe the vibrant interaction of Heaven, Earth, and humans in a Confucian worldview.[39] In this context, humans complete the natural and cosmic world by becoming participants in the dynamic transfomative life processes. This idea can extend ethics to apply to the land-species-human-planet-universe continuum.

As Tu Weiming observes for the Confucian tradition:

> Human beings are . . . an integral part of the 'chain of being', encompassing Heaven, Earth, and the myriad things. However, the uniqueness of being human is the

intrinsic capacity of the mind to 'embody' (*ti*) the cosmos in its conscience and consciousness. Through this embodying, the mind realizes its own sensitivity, manifests true humanity and assists in the cosmic transformation of Heaven and Earth.[40]

This cosmic transformation implies that humans have a special role in being aligned with the fecund, nourishing powers of life. They need to be responsive to other humans but also to the larger macrocosm of the universe in which humans are a microcosm. This is clearly expressed by the Neo-Confucian thinker Zhang Zai in his renowned essay "The Western Inscription" which hung on the western wall of his study:

> Heaven is my father and Earth is my mother, and even such a small creature as I finds an intimate place in their midst.
>
> Therefore that which extends throughout the universe I regard as my body and that which directs the universe I consider as my nature.
>
> All people are my brothers and sisters, and all things are my companions.
>
> . . . Respect the aged . . . Show affection toward the orphaned and the weak . . . the sage identifies his virtue with that of Heaven and Earth . . . Even those who are tired and infirm, crippled or sick, those who have no brothers or children, wives or husbands, are all my brothers who are in distress and have no one to turn to.
>
> . . . one who puts his moral nature into practice and brings his physical existence to complete fulfillment can match [Heaven and Earth] . . . and one who penetrates

spirit to the highest degree will skillfully carry out their will.[41]

The Comprehensive Context: Restoration of Wonder

*I*f our optimal role as humans is to be creative participants within cosmological processes, how can the world's religions foster that role? The religions have been challenged over the last several centuries by major revolutions in the understanding of the role of humans in relation to science, politics, economics, and society. Some may see the ecological revolution as just another step in these significant movements in human history and consciousness. However, we might observe that this is more than simply a slight shift of perspective. It is rather a major transformation that involves both effort and evocation. It requires a comprehensive re-visioning of what it is to be human on a finite planet amidst infinite immensities. We have the possibility to envision ourselves now not only as political, economic, or social beings, but also as planetary beings embedded in and dependent on nature's seasons, cycles, and resources. Although urban living and modernity have removed many humans from this direct experience, it has not lessened our capacity for biophilia, as E.O. Wilson suggests, or for a deep sense of renewal and wonder in contact with nature's rhythms. Through science we understand that we are cosmological beings within a vast evolutionary universe and now have a responsibility, in some way, for the integrity and stability of these life processes.

Religions have historically served as a means of channeling the hopes and aspirations of humans toward a larger vision of their place and purpose. Now religions are challenged to provide a more comprehensive narrative perspective for situating human life in relation to our finite planet. The renewing energies that ground and dynamize the human spirit must be brought forward. For millennia, these energies have provided the spiritual orientations of the world's civilizations and cultures. Religions have traditionally been a means of expanding the measure of the mind through the power of the religious imagination; now is the moment for the religions to move forward boldly with comprehensive narrative perspectives that are grounded in relevant traditional resources, open to a sense of wonder, and guided by inspiring moral visions for shaping human-Earth relations for a sustainable future.

In this spirit, the religions of the world are moving into their ecological phase and finding their planetary expression. This is their fundamental challenge in relation to the environmental crisis. Can the religious traditions awaken a renewed sense of awe and reverence for the Earth as a numinous matrix of mystery? Can they activate the depths of resonance in the human that will resound with the awesome beauty of the universe? Can they open a space for our participation in the life processes that is healing and renewing for human-Earth relations? Can they raise key ethical questions regarding the destruction of the environment, and at the same time provide resources of inspiration that will sustain the energies needed to preserve, protect, and restore the environment? Can the religious traditions speak effectively to the contemporary world while challenging the limits of modernity as well?

These are their challenges and indeed all of our challenges as we begin to take on our cosmological being, to dwell in intimate immensities. We are cracking open the shell of our anthropocentric selves and our particular religious traditions to move toward more expansive religious sensibilities that embrace both Earth and universe. New configurations of tradition and modernity will emerge, and with them will come retrieval of texts, reconstruction of theologies, renewal of symbols and rituals, re-evaluation of ethics, and, most importantly, a revivified sense of wonder and celebration.

Central to this great transformation of the religions into their ecological phase is the reawakening in the human of a sense of awe and wonder regarding the beauty, complexity, and mystery of life itself. Rachel Carson highlighted this many years ago in her reflections on *A Sense of Wonder*.[42] In his book, *The Tangled Wing*, the anthropologist and neurologist, Melvin Konner, calls for this recovery of wonder:

It seems to me we are losing the sense of wonder, the hallmark of our species and the central feature of the human spirit. Perhaps this is due to the depredations of science and technology against the arts and humanities, but I doubt it—although this is certainly something to be concerned about. I suspect it is simply that the human spirit is insufficiently developed at this moment in evolution, much like the wing of *Archaeopteryx*. Whether we can free it for further development will depend, in part, on the full reinstatement of the sense of wonder.[43]

Will the world's religions assist in the further development of the human spirit as they have throughout their long, unfolding journey to the present? If religions are vessels for nurturing the sense of the sacred, surely they will continue to respond to the sacred that is manifest in the wonder of life and in its continuity. If indigenous traditions have sustained human-Earth relations for some 150,000 years, surely their traditional environmental knowledge and sense of awe in the presence of nature will continue to contribute to the future of the Earth community. If the human mind and spirit has created compelling and coherent visions to inspire the flourishing of civilizations for the last five thousand years, surely that same rich and diverse religious imagination will continue to activate the energies and commitments needed to sustain life on the planet. These are our collective tasks; these are our particular challenges.

Those energies and commitments will depend in large part on the measure and magnitude of the awe and wonder we evoke. And let us remember it is not only awe and wonder but also dread and terror that awakens the human imagination and lies at the heart of the burning bush. That which is numinous attracts us and repels us, as Rudolph Otto reminds us.[44] Nature is filled with awesome mystery, with beauty and death inextricably intertwined. Will the fire consume us or transform us? Will it ignite worldly wonder?

Commentary by
Judith A. Berling

PROFESSOR TUCKER'S LECTURE, although graciously worded and graciously delivered, is befitting for Christians in the Lenten season, for it calls us to serious self-reflection and a turning away (repentance) from long established habits of thought and action. Although the lecture is particularly seasonal for Christians, it is in fact addressed equally to adherents of all religions. It is an important and significant message that I pray we may be ready to hear. It is a message particularly challenging for North Americans, who are profoundly attached to a standard and style of living that threatens the survival of human populations in poverty-stricken areas of the world as well as of biological species and irreplaceable natural resources throughout the world.

Professor Tucker briefly describes the ecological crisis, and then articulates the ways in which the world's religions (including Christianity) can offer resources to respond to it, providing not only articulations of values higher than consumption and accumulation, but also the moral authority to inspire human beings to change their ways of living for the sake of the long-term survival of our species, all species, and the planet. This is the good news.

The bad news is that there are significant challenges for each of the religions in "stepping up to the plate" on this issue. Let me review a few of these in ways that I hope will stimulate response and discussion by this audience.

First, Tucker joins Joanna Macy and others calling religions into their planetary or Gaia phase: "Just as they have been working in the twentieth century to embrace diversity within the human community, so now they are called to embrace the vast diversity of life in the Earth community." The challenge here is that we have to admit that our twentieth-century work is far from complete: the embrace of diversity within the human community remains unfinished as long as the specters of racism, sexism, homophobia, and other forms of unjust discrimination haunt us. So, we can't simply say, "Well, now we've handled human diversity, it's time to move on to diversity of life in the Earth community." Moreover, the long and hard struggles for human justice remind us that the struggle for biojustice or geojustice will also be vexing and difficult. From a Christian perspective, human sinfulness is a deeply rooted and stubborn enemy.

Second, it is a great challenge to reconcile the worldviews of the various religions with a view that calls human beings to their responsibilities for sustaining the planet in its biodiversity. This requires some fundamental rethinking of religious cosmologies and religious anthropologies. John Cobb and others have argued that Process Theology is promising for Christians in this regard, but that itself is a challenge, since Process Theology has not been a dominant (or even prominent) theological discourse.[45]

Third, Professor Tucker argues that the ecological crisis is more than simply one more issue, and yet religious thought does not start from this crisis. The thinking of all religions begins somewhere else, and works its way to the relations of human life to all life on the planet by a rather long and tortuous road. I admit that I have a hard time envisioning how this issue will move front and center in the thinking of any of the religions: that is to say, we may worry about our "primary" issues within each of the religions while the planet dies around us.

Fourth, Professor Tucker acknowledges the disjunction between tradition and modernity, but argues rightly that religions are never static, that they respond to challenges and change over time. However, they tend to respond very slowly indeed, and too often their first response to challenge is to turn back to tradition, where "sureties" are to be found. The strength of fundamentalisms in various religions both around the globe and here in the United States are ample testimony to this. How are the more "liberal" voices of the various religions to find their authority in the face of terrifying challenges that seem to require fundamental rethinking of the "verities" and patterns of virtually all religions?

Fifth, who is to take the lead in this dialogue? The persons perhaps best prepared and most motivated to enter into a dialogue with other faiths and other disciplines (economics, the sciences, and so forth) are the academics, who are more likely to have the training to participate in such multifaceted conversations. But, at least in our culture, will the academics have any power or influence to motivate the changes required to save the planet—changes either within the religious communities or within society? I see two major problems: 1. Academic dialogues tend to become very sophisticated, but as they do so, they become less comprehensible and accessible to a general audience, or the media. 2. Academics often fail to see the gap between ideas and actions, cited by Professor Tucker in her lecture. How are dialogues among academics going to be linked to actions which might change the course of planetary destruction? Are we as academics ready and willing to link our discussions to practical actions and policies, and then to communicate our ideas and effect changes within the religious communities and within society?

Finally, the changes required of North Americans will mandate a significant change in lifestyle to embrace moderation and simplicity rather than unfettered growth and accumulation. The economic and political "engines" of this society are powerfully arrayed against such a change—so powerfully that embracing a life of genuine moderation and simplicity is no easy matter in this culture. (Many of us may believe we live a moderate or simple life compared to others in the United States, but on a global scale our level of consumption is still extremely high.) Does religion (and today it would have to be a strong coalition of the many religions represented in the culture) have the moral authority, the voice, and the clout to move us toward such a change? What would it take to develop such authority, voice, and clout?

The six difficulties I have posed are not a criticism of Professor Tucker's premises, or of her belief that religion can be a significant contributor to addressing the ecological crisis. On the contrary, I believe that she is entirely correct. What I give voice to is my deep concern about how challenging it will be for all of the religions. It is my hope and my prayer that participants in all religious communities will recognize the ecological crisis and the importance of addressing it— that each religion will be willing to recognize ways in which its tradition has contributed to the crisis, and to articulate values and strategies to change human behavior into planetarily as well as humanly compassionate behavior.

Response and Audience Discussion

MARY EVELYN TUCKER: I agree with Judith Berling that there is still much to be done regarding justice in the human community. As I have tried to suggest in my talk, there is an important continuity between social and ecological issues. We can no longer afford to address them as separate. The liberation of humans and the protection of the planet can be seen as part of a larger movement of the creation of an integral Earth community.

The liberating impulses of the Enlightenment for human dignity, political democracy, and societal equity certainly need to be continued and extended to many parts of the world. At the same time, there is an overwhelming realization that the unlimited extension of human freedom along with economic drive and resource exploitation has compromised the development of community and ecosystems on many levels. The grounding of our human aspirations within the creativity of Earth processes and within the limits of ecosystems may give some appropriate measure to the expansive tendencies of the Enlightenment mentality. As we recognize more fully that humans are a subsystem of the Earth, we may have the basis for establishing equitable and sustainable economic, social, and political systems. To do this we need to develop new forms of eco-economics, eco-justice, and eco-democracy for the Earth community. Unless we sustain the basis of all life systems our efforts at justice for humans alone will be severely undermined.

An example of the alliance of liberating concerns for humans and for the Earth can be seen in ecofeminism. The voices of women, in particular, should be encouraged and supported against those repressive patriarchal forces often embedded in cultural attitudes and reinforced by religion. At the same time the liberating voices of women can also be seen in connection with the liberation of the Earth. Ecofeminism is making a distinctive contribution to this intricate alignment of ecological and feminist concerns.

In this same spirit, we need to see the call to respect biodiversity as in alignment with the call to respect cultural diversity. Indeed, preserving cultural diversity often depends on preserving biodiversity, for example, as in the intricate relations of native peoples to plants and animals in ceremonial and ritual life as well as in subsistence practices. The various types and colors of corn for the Hopi Indians are essential to their culture and their livelihood. Similarly, the Imara Indians of Bolivia and Peru have developed complex patterns of relationship between numerous forms of maize and potatoes. With the disappearance of species or pollution of bioregions, indigenous cultures are particularly vulnerable to erosion of cultural habits and values. For example, the presence of persistent organic pollutants (POPs) in the Arctic region has had devastating effects on animals and cultures. As seals, walruses, polar bears, and whales show signs of increasing contamination, so too does this effect the peoples who rely on these animals for food, clothing, and shelter.

RETHINKING RELIGIOUS COSMOLOGIES AND ANTHROPOLOGIES

I agree with Judith that calling humans to be responsible for creating the conditions for sustainablity will be a significant challenge for religious cosmologies. This has been one of the primary concerns of indigenous traditions for thousands of years. For most of the other religious traditions it will require rethinking of their cosmologies and anthropologies. This is in fact already happening with religions that are beginning to absorb a sense of evolutionary history and to rethink their own anthropocentric perspectives in light of ecological concerns. It is also the case that many religious cosmologies and anthropologies have implicit or explicit resources illustrating how humans are part of nature and thus concerned for its continuity and well being. Identifying these cosmologies and anthropologies is a large part of the motivation behind the Harvard conferences and books on world religions and ecology.

Most religious cosmologies begin with an origin story that describes how the universe was born and what our role is in this world. While it is true that there is an other-worldly impulse in many of the world's religions, that is rarely the exclusive thrust of the traditions. In fact, the rich symbolic imaginations evident in scriptures and in ritual practices of the world's religions abundantly reflect nature's processes. The magnificence of the seasons and cycles of nature are present in scriptures such as the Psalms in Judaism, the parables in Christianity, the *Vedas* in Hinduism, and the *Book of Changes* (*I Ching*) in Confucianism and Daoism. Commentaries on these scriptures in light of ecological sensibilities will be helpful in extending the import of scripture for contemporary circumstances. By the same token, rituals which embody and celebrate nature's variety, complexity, and powers of renewal include hunting rituals in indigenous traditions, agricultural rituals such as rice planting in Shinto, and harvest thanksgiving ceremonies such as *Sukhot* in Judaism. Moreover, the whole liturgical cycles of Judaism and of Christianity are in consonance with the seasonal cycles of agricultural societies reflecting the fecundity of nature in its "death" and "rebirth" patterns. Awareness of these deep connections to nature in ritual can be revitalized.

Thus it is not only to Whiteheadian versions of process thought that we can turn for cosmologies that have ecological implications. Rather, it is also to retrieving and renewing appropriate cosmologies and anthropologies that are already explicit or implicit in the world's religions.

WHERE DOES RELIGIOUS THINKING BEGIN?

Judith rightly observes that religious thought does not begin with the ecological crisis and that this will be difficult to bring to the center of attention for religions. It will indeed be a challenge but not one that it is altogether insurmountable. It is true that when the indigenous traditions arose and later when the world's religious and philosophical thought came into being one could not even conceive of a planetary crisis such as we are now facing. The religions are thus necessary but not sufficient to the task of transformation at hand. Clearly this is why we need a multidisciplinary approach involving science, social science, and humanities.

However, it is not fully accurate to claim that "all religions begin somewhere else" and work their way to the life of the planet. If what is implied here is that most religions are originally concerned with personal salvation, that may be said of the western traditions but not of all religions. Certainly indigenous traditions around the planet have been centered on the life of nature as a primary source of religious inspiration. The profound recognition of the dependence of humans on nature for subsistence becomes the basis for ritual and ceremonial life of indigenous peoples. They begin with gratitude for the animals, fish, plants, grains, water, soil, and sunshine that sustain life and livelihood. Moreover, the traditions of East Asia (Confucianism,

Daoism, and Shinto) as well as the East Asian forms of Buddhism (such as Chan and Hua Yan) have a fully developed cosmological sense of nature. The natural world is seen not simply as background, but as that with which one harmonizes oneself as a means of spiritual cultivation. The fecundity and rhythms of nature as expressed in the Dao pervade Confucian and Daoist thought. Indeed, this world-affirming sensibility transformed Buddhism into its Chinese forms of Chan and Hua Yan.

I want to return to Judith's point that the planet may die around us while the religions are preoccupied with internal issues. That is certainly a probability. There is, however, an urgency and ultimacy about the possibility of biocide that haunts us and calls the religions to a reawakening. There are signs that this is beginning to occur. Although many traditions are preoccupied with internal issues of survival, it may well be that in responding to the ecological crisis the religions themselves may be renewed. The movement of religions into their ecological phase is thus a means of transforming and extending their spiritual vision and direction for the future of life on the planet. This may not only be an intellectual option, but also a revivifying choice for the religious traditions to embrace the community of life with comprehensive moral imagination. In so doing, the traditions themselves may be revitalized.

THE CHALLENGE OF RELIGIOUS FUNDAMENTALISM

Judith's comments on fundamentalism are insightful, and various forms of fundamentalism are clearly flourishing around the planet. It is also true that religions have indeed changed over time in both ideas and practices. There is ample testimony to this fact, for example, in the broadening of social concerns from the powerful support that many religious movements have given originally to caring for the sick, the elderly, the infirm and later to providing shelter for orphans, homes for children, education for the next generation, and, in the twentieth century, lending support to farmers and laborers, and in recent years to women and minorities. All of these are examples of where religions have been active in the social sphere—often over opposition from the more entrenched forces in society.

It's true that "fundamentalisms" have arisen throughout the world religions over the history of their development. This is, I think, an inevitable aspect of the dialectical processes of conservative and liberalizing forces which are part of the development of institutions and ideas over time. Thus, the interaction of tradition and modernity are processes of the creative intersection of continuity and change of ideas and practice, which lend vitality to the movements of history and culture. Dynamic new syntheses inevitably arise from these exchanges and interactions.

The widespread presence of fundamentalisms in various parts of the globe is an indication of these processes at work. With rapid modernization, globalization, and secularization taking place, traditional religious thought and practice have been severely undermined. As people are thrust into the modern world with ever-greater speed, they seek anchors of security and fixity in the past. Fundamentalisms are such anchors as people long for assurance in the midst of uncertainty and change.

The liberalizing voices are challenged to be ever more clear, articulate, and persuasive in relation to the various forms of fundamentalisms that oppose their views. This is in some ways a fortunate inevitability of the manner in which ideas and attitudes move forward across the currents of time and history. Fundamentalisms or opposing viewpoints provide the occasion for more clearly thought out positions regarding the contributions of world religions to ecological concerns. Because this is a defining moment for the world's religions, clear and comprehensive reflection will be needed along with the appropriate transforming action. Simplistic solutions, sectarian rhetoric, or self-serving action will be inadequate for the tasks ahead. Carefully honing the voices of religions may be a valuable part of the process.

It's also true that we need not see these movements of "conservative fundamentalism" and "progressive liberalism" as black-and-white oppositions. More complex readings and analyses need to be done regarding the spectrum of positions that are being articulated within religions and between religions. The word "conservation" itself implies conserving what is valuable in nature and by extension here conserving what is valuable in tradition. This is also the intent of the Harvard project. Thus we suggest there needs to be retrieval of religious resources, re-evaluation of what will be most helpful, and renewal and reconstruction of traditions.

An example of the more complex reality of conserving religious traditions in relation to the modern world arose in the Tehran Seminar on Environment Culture and Religion in June 2001, sponsored by the Islamic Republic of Iran and the United Nations Environment Programme. The Iranian government has a statement in its constitution highlighting the support of Islamic teachings for environmental protection. There is a widespread realization by government officials and religious leaders that this may be a key means of raising ecological consciousness in the region. Iran and other areas of the Middle East have been devastated by drought in the last several years and many leaders are conscious of how severe the situation is when cities such as Tehran, with twelve million people, often have water for only eight hours a day.

WHO WILL TAKE THE LEAD IN INTER-RELIGIOUS DIALOGUE ON THE ENVIRONMENT?

Judith raises the question of whether academics are up to the task. We conceived this Harvard project on religion and ecology as not simply one of academics talking with other academics, but rather as a project that deepens and expands the religious discourse so as to contribute to effective environmental policies and persuasive environmental ethics on issues affecting the future of the planet. We envision the project in a series on concentric circles that allows for the translation of ideas generated by the conferences and books to reach a wider audience. From its conception the project embraced both ideas and practices in varied publications that are accessible to academics and to non-academics.

Such a deepening of the discourse within each of the religious traditions and a broadening of the dialogue across traditions in addressing environmental issues have involved a major collaborative effort of scholars of religious studies. We are identifying a remarkably rich core of religious resources in this ten-volume Harvard book series, which will help to open up a field of study for future research in colleges, universities, and seminaries. This has been a scholarly endeavor but in conjunction with environmentalists who participated in the conference series. For a broadly educated public we have also published a synthesizing issue on religion and ecology in the journal *Daedalus* (Fall 2001). See www.daedalus.amacad.org /issues/fall2001/fall2001. This volume brings together scholars of the world's religions with thoughtful voices from science, ethics, education, and policy around the problem of global climate change.

We are conscious, however, that these concepts need to be made accessible beyond academia. Thus we have done publications to translate these ideas outward for use in seminaries, churches, synagogues, temples, and community groups. These publications include an issue of *Earth Ethics* in 1998 and a book on *Earth and Faith* in 2000 done for the United Nations Environment Programme that highlights key environmental problems such as water, oceans, climate change, and biodiversity. In addition, we are reaching beyond colleges and universities to secondary schools. For the last several years we have been organizing multidisciplinary workshops at the request of high school teachers. The younger generation both in high school and in college genuinely seems to understand and to be excited by this emerging field of religion and ecology. In fact, many of these students want to study it further on the graduate level so as to make contributions to a more sustainable future. In addition to making a variety of publications available, we hope to continue the interfacing of academics with those in science and public policy who welcome the ethical voices on these issues regarding the environment.

MODERATION AND SIMPLICITY VERSUS GROWTH AND ACCUMULATION

It is true, as Judith suggests, that movements toward moderation of lifestyle within the developed world—especially the United States—will be significant both symbolically and practically. The book on *Voluntary Simplicity* by Duane Elgin has sparked significant interest in this regard. Nonetheless, consumption habits are difficult to break, especially when driven by advertising, media, and cultural pressures for status. The growing gap between rich and poor is a cause of concern both as a matter of equity and as that which breeds resentment, encourages migrations, and fuels terrorism. This gap is especially visible between the developed and developing world. However, it is also present within the developing world itself as pockets of wealth stand in stark contrast to huge cities teeming with dispossessed migrants, unemployed workers, and homeless people.

Do religions have the moral authority to urge change in this regard? Liberation theology in Latin America is one example of the significant work of theologians and lay people to highlight the teachings of Christianity as being in solidarity with the needs of the poor. The efforts to preach this gospel of the dispossessed in word and in deed have been widespread and, by many measures, quite effective in shifting the focus of the Latin American churches. Clearly much still remains to be done in this regard—

in Latin America, in Africa, and in Asia by many of the world's religions.

In North America movements to shift patterns of consumerism and to make businesses more ecologically responsive have begun in several quarters. The Center for a New American Dream represents such a move, as does a wide range of business efforts such as the Global Reporting Initiative (GRI). The question is to what extent religions may be aligned with these movements or inspire future movements. At this juncture it is probably more accurate to say that some leaders of these movements may have been inspired in part by religious values—for example, Robert Massie, the head of CERES is an Episcopal priest. There are certainly growing movements within churches to live more sustainably in terms of supporting recycling and alternative green energy programs. Much more can be done in this regard.

What will it take for religions to develop the moral authority, voice and clout? It may necessitate a further turning of religious institutions themselves to a simpler lifestyle and green living. It will require new kinds of coalitions of religious leaders and lay people, theologians and scholars of comparative religions to articulate a convincing vision and an achievable plan of action. In addition, it will be strengthened by alliances with environmentalists who recognize the value of authentic voices of moral persuasion. Such coalitions and alliances have enormous potential for transformation if we hope to achieve the grounds for a sustainable future.

DISCUSSION WITH AUDIENCE

QUESTION: When it comes to the United Nations and the various resources that they can marshal, there's a building, there's a schedule, there's an address, there are translation facilities, there all the NGOs and all the constituents back home. Ideas can be disseminated in a variety of languages very quickly. When it comes to religions coming together to speak unequivocally, there's no building, there's no table, there's no translation facility, there's no fundamental agreement even within denominations about what might be their faith-tradition's approach to environmental crises, or what resources they might muster to respond to technological challenges. I would love to be encouraged that religions can contribute, but what have you seen, or where would you look, to bring religions together in their environmental expression in this ecological age?

TUCKER'S RESPONSE: That's a very important question. As you suggest, it may be helpful to have an international organization that would bring the religions of the world together in an effective manner-especially around environmental issues. On the other hand, we need to be duly cautious as we know that such bureaucracies have their limitations and forming new institutions is enormously time-consuming and resource-draining. In addition, one of the practical limits is that the world's religions (unlike the nation states) don't have the same kinds of political structures to represent their varied constituencies.

We do, however, have some models of international organizations or conferences of world religions. One is the Parliament of World Religions that held its first meeting in Chicago in 1893. It did not meet again until one hunbdred years later, also in Chicago, and then in 1999 in Cape Town, South Africa. The next Parliament will be in 2004 in Barcelona. While this is a loosely structured organization it has been effective in highlighting environmental concerns along with social justice and peace as primary challenges for the religions to address. The World Conference on Religion and Peace (WCRP) based in New York has also been effective in the arena of peace and conflict resolution. In recent years, the United Religions Initiative (URI) headquartered in San Francisco has begun to encourage grassroots inter-religious networking around the world.

These organizations will continue to play important roles in bringing together the world's religions around significant topics. With regard to the environment and the world's religions there is a need to deepen the discourse of the religious communities. In this way they will be able to move beyond mere rhetoric or a sense of sectarian self-satisfaction which is often evident in national and international conferences on the environment where religious leaders or lay people have been present. This deepening of the discourse within each of the religious traditions and the broadening of the dialogue across traditions in addressing environmental issues has been the object of the Harvard conferences and book series on world religions and ecology. This is a major collaborative effort of scholars from the field of religious studies that is beginning to have an impact on policy.

There are many other angles for religions to enter this conversation on the environment and a sustainable future and to make effective use of their institutional power and presence. I find it particularly striking that doors one might think would be closed to religions are in fact opening. The doors of the United Nations are one example, especially through the United Nations Environment Programme (UNEP). The director of UNEP, Klaus Topfer, realizes that religions can make a real contribution in this arena. He has encouraged those voices in several international conferences. The scientific door is another. Religions need to realize there's more opportunity for collaboration with science than what might have previously been thought. In 1998 we went to the American Museum of Natural History in New York to explore holding a culminating conference there which would conclude the Harvard series of ten conferences on the world's religions and ecology. We wanted to bring together representatives of the world's religions and representatives from other disciplines working on the environment. The museum's Provost, Michael Novacek, who I thought would be a gray-haired elderly man in a conservative suit, was a brilliant longhaired scientist who studies the evolution of birds and dinosaurs in the Mongolian desert. Within five minutes into our conversation he said, "You don't have to convince me of the importance of the role of religion. In fact, the need for this role has become quite apparent to some of the museum's curators. We have just hired an ornithologist, and four of the six final candidates had watched their birds go extinct while they were studying them." He acknowledged that this was a significant wake-up call for the museum and its mission. Indeed, he observed: "We realized we needed to encourage ethical voices regarding the environmental devastation that is taking place."

There are indeed fascinating and unexpected openings occurring for dialogue with religions and we need to see where we can go through the doors to move this conversation forward.

QUESTION: We are talking about very large and complex systems—I liked the way you phrased it earlier: "Even scientists don't have a complete handle on some of these issues." I would say, *especially* scientists don't have a handle on these issues. At the same time, I wonder who should have the authority to implement the changes the environmental crisis requires? In our society, there is a division between the rule of law (secular law and government) and the influence of religious institutions. This represents a relatively new but effective arrangement. It implies a clear distinction between the rule of law and a moral force. In my opinion, the role of organized religions is to nurture and influence consciousness so that people develop their own ability to grasp these issues and to apply them to their own lives. It is not the role of organized religions, however, to implement these changes. Organized religions ought, in my opinion, to continue to do what they have always done: inspire and inform the individual conscience. It is up to the secular institutions to do what they do, namely, make laws and implement policy. We don't need to be anxious about the fact that organized religions lack the authority or agency to effect widespread change (as the earlier question implied). Don't you think that organized religion should vigorously do what it does best—to envision and articulate the right path, and quietly support, not direct its course? Shouldn't that be left to our secular institutions?

TUCKER'S RESPONSE: That is definitely a complex statement and question that requires further clarification and elaboration than I can go into here. Briefly, yes, religions need to do what they can do well, namely articulate an inspiring moral vision for human-Earth relations that will not allow us to simply witness the death of many forms of life on the planet. At the same time, we need to respect the separation of church and state as it has emerged in post-Enlightenment democracies. All of that is extremely important. On the other hand, I think we would agree that law itself is certainly not uninfluenced by religious ethics and moral concerns.

Moreover, what I am suggesting is that we are in the midst of a transformation of all disciplines—science, humanities, social sciences—and that this multidisciplinary shift is certainly taking place in law as well. Environmental law, for example, is a new phase of law that we didn't even recognize twenty-five years ago, and certainly didn't evoke in the way we do now. The growing field of environmental ethics has clearly influenced environmental law. Moral principles, environmental ethics, and law are coming together in significant ways.

For example, on an international level, the Earth Charter is a soft-law document, namely, a statement of principles that serves as a moral compass for sustainable development. The International Union for the Conversation of Nature (IUCN) has negotiated a comprehensive covenant of environmental laws to support these principles through enforcement. This illustrates how jurisprudence is clearly moving to another level of its own expression regarding the "rights of nature." It's part of this larger shift toward the formation of an Earth Community in which the religions are beginning to participate.

QUESTION: I'd like to ask Professor Tucker to respond perhaps in a different way as a follow up to the last questioner's suggestion that religions should "stay out of it," so to speak. When you spoke earlier about ways in which religions had become involved in issues in the past, I immediately thought of the civil rights movement in this country—a movement led by religious leaders and one born and sustained by a religious impetus. I wonder if you could talk a bit more about how the world's religions can overcome some of their internal blocks to becoming bioethical. I'm sure you've struggled with these issues. What kind of scenario do you imagine that could stir the kind of passion that lay behind the civil rights movement? What could sweep religions into that same kind of energy and concern with regard to ecological problems?

TUCKER'S RESPONSE: Again that's a wonderful question and an excellent point that religions were very active in the civil rights movement in this country and certainly in the anti-Vietnam War movement as well. I went to college in Washington, D.C., and was an active participant in the civil rights marches and the demonstrations against the Vietnam War. These were often conducted with extraordinary leadership of many from the religious community. Martin Luther King, Jr., Daniel and Philip Berrigan and others with strong religious sensibilities for civil rights and peace are noteworthy examples. As you observe, there was a powerful religious impetus behind these movements. One can describe this as an impetus for justice which is especially pronounced in the Jewish, Christian, and

Islamic traditions. I am suggesting that concern for the environment is another dimension of that transformation of social and political consciousness that has moved forward with the support of religious leaders and communities. I see this as part of a continuity of concerns for the future of humans in alignment with other species and ecosystems. This evokes an expansion of ethical sensibilities as reflected in terms such as "human-Earth relations." Thus many in the religious communities are now calling for eco-justice or environmental justice. Chet Bowers's book *Educating for Eco-Justice and Community* (University of Georgia Press, 2001) illustrates the need to make the connections with social justice and environmental issues. All of this implies a profound and renewing realization that humans are a subset of the Earth and dependent on the Earth for our life and sustenance.

You are asking as well, what will it take for the deep passion for environmental transformation to be stirred? We can say there are at least two ways. One possibility is that environmental disasters will bring forth the passion, although I'd rather not think of it in that particular way. Nonetheless, we are facing environmental catastrophes on many fronts, some more visible than others. It is clear, for example, that we are living in a period of the greatest migrations in human history and much of this is due to environmental degradation. Forty million people a year are migrating and as a result megacities of almost unlivable conditions are emerging in Asia, Africa, and

Latin America. This should evoke some passion about environmentally sustainable futures for these migrants and their families.

Another way to evoke environmental passion in a positive sense is through the comprehensive perspective of evolution as articulated by Brian Swimme and Thomas Berry in their book *The Universe Story*. This deep sense of our connection to a vast universe process has the potential to open our imagination to the sacredness and beauty of this cosmic, evolutionary journey that I referred to at the beginning of my talk. In awakening this deep feeling of connection, we can tap into the sustaining energies for living in alignment with earth's processes, seasons, cycles, and ecosystems.

And I believe those same kinds of Earth-connecting energies are beginning to arise anew in the religious communities and to be expressed in practical programs. We can highlight many environmental projects around the world that are inspired by religious convictions regarding the sacredness of life and the need for restraint in use of resources. Here in the United States the Global Climate Change Campaign of the National Council of Churches in conjunction with the Coalition for Environment and Jewish Life has been extraordinarily effective and quite outspoken. It has elicited letters with signatures from major religious leaders across North America directed to President Bush to say that global climate change is a moral issue and that the poor will especially suffer as climate change becomes increasingly dramatized. Another example is the Episcopal Power and Light Project founded by Sally Bingham and Steve MacAusland. This has received tremendous attention and shows concretely how religious communities can participate in the use of renewable energy.

In these examples we are talking about more sustainable uses of physical energy that won't pollute the environment. We are at the end of the petroleum era. As Thomas Berry says in *The Great Work* we are participating in the "petroleum interval." Within fifty years all these kinds of configurations of petroleum-based energy will be changed in life-altering ways. The religious community is well placed to begin to illustrate how these changes are going to affect all of us, but particularly the poor. In the international community there is already a sophisticated understanding of the intricate connection between poverty, development, and the environment that has drawn in the religious voices. Because poverty and development have been concerns of the religious community over the last several decades, the linkage to the environment is just another step forward. The passion for speaking out on these issues is definitely emerging in the religious communities and can be connected to the international community and NGO networks in this area.

QUESTION: I would like to follow up on the previous questions a little bit. Various people have suggested that religion is responsible in some part for the environmental crisis that we are in. For example, Lynn White's essay published in *Science* in 1967 on the religious roots of environmental exploitation makes this argument. You mentioned a number of things in this regard. One is that religions are changing and we are evolving into a new ecological age in religion. You also mentioned the problem of consumption and how we need to reassess our place in the world. If we think of religion as fundamentally the transformation of the heart, how do you think this new period of religions, with the new connection to the environment, can help with the problem of the transformation of the heart so we are not so sucked into the material world and all of the problems that causes for the environment?

TUCKER'S RESPONSE: Again, a superb and insightful question regarding an issue that I think is so much at the heart of these matters. Materialism and consumerism—and what John Cobb calls "economism" linked with "globalization"—is a major challenge. Judith Berling identified this very clearly in her question on lifestyles in the United States. When we are talking about consumption and the use of resources, we know that we in the United States account for only four or five percent of the world's population, yet we are using twenty-five percent of the world's resources. This is just astounding. We can see this with regard to oil use, especially in our resistance to driving smaller and more fuel-efficient cars. Without being simplistic about it (because the issues are extremely complex and can be addressed in a number of ways) a counterpoint to the addiction of materialism is not necessarily telling people what they should do. Nor is it making them feel filled with guilt more than they already are for what's wrong with the world or what's wrong with them.

I would suggest that a counterpoint to addictive materialism is evoking both understanding and wonder that assists us in seeing ourselves as part of the vast processes that have sustained life on the planet. Understanding Earth processes and their extraordinarily delicate and complex components makes us realize that we are part of an intricate web of creative life forces. Moreover, these natural processes are ways in which modes of divine presence become clarified in our mind, body, and spirit. So the question is how do we also evoke wonder regarding the world that has heart-transforming potential. Wonder and understanding are what elicits and ignites in humans something of their participation in this process of life that transcends words, yet creates a deeply felt resonance that inspires action. Such an experience of resonance with life can surely affect the kinds of transformation away from materialism and toward creativity that many of us imagine is possible.

QUESTION: When I think of environmental degradation I think of not only individual lifestyles and personal choices, but also of large institutions like corporations and governments with their military policies that create a lot of environmental devastation. My question is: To what extent do you see religions and initiatives involving multiple religious faiths presenting some kind of focused critique of economic systems that allow that kind of degradation to take place, or perhaps incur that kind of degradation? I am referring not necessarily to focused critiques of capitalism, but critiques of the profit motive and the ways that contributes to environmental degradation.

TUCKER'S RESPONSE: As you suggest, the changes many of us envision will require not only rethinking individual lifestyles but also making larger structural changes. This involves a whole new understanding of ecological economics that encourages us to see the Earth not simply as commodity but as community, not simply as resource but as source of life. Herman Daly, Richard Norgaard, Robert Costanza, Paul Hawkins, Lester Brown, Neva Goodwin, and Juliet Schor and others are pointing the way toward such ecological economics.

This perspective is far removed from the pervasive corporate view of profit at any cost where the bottom line does not take into account the depletion of Earth's resources or pollution of its ecosystems. The consequent transformation of human energies into processes involving production and consumption as the main direction of human endeavors is very much at the base of many of our current problems. And the other area that you identify—the government and the military—really needs to be addressed with regard to environmental degradation. The clean up of toxic waste on military installations in this country is estimated to cost well over twenty billion dollars. One of my colleagues at Bucknell University has been a consultant for the government on the studies for Yucca Mountain in Nevada to be used as a national repository for nuclear waste. The studies alone have taken up some six billion dollars over a decade. All of this is virtually invisible in terms of the reported costs of a military presence and of nuclear energy.

In terms of who is addressing these issues from within the religious community, a number of Christian theologians are doing an extraordinary job of critiquing "economism" in its various forms: homogenizing globalization, exploitative processes of extraction, profit creation that overrides social justice, and wealth making that causes severe inequities. The theologian John Cobb wrote a book with the economist Herman Daly called *For the Common Good* addressing many of these questions. Sallie McFague, a feminist theologian, has continued this critique in her latest book, *Life Abundant* (Minneapolis: Fortress Press, 2001) and in her article in the *Christianity and Ecology* volume from Harvard Press where she speaks of the need to address this mindless economic drive. Another hopeful sign is a movement which was begun by an Episcopal Minister, Robert Massie, called CERES—the Coalition for Environmentally Responsible Economies. CERES has received significant funding from the United Nations Foundation and from corporate sources. They have compiled an impressive list of corporations to sign on to an environmental mission statement based on the Valdez Principles. I think these are important signs of change, although clearly more needs to be done.

We have a professor here tonight from the Haas School of Business at the University of California at Berkeley who might like to speak to this topic.

COMMENT: My name is Jack Philips. I would just mention that, at the Haas School of Business, ethics has been a required component of the graduate program—although only one unit—for maybe six or seven years. That program has been expanding somewhat. More interestingly, in the undergraduate program, there is a new ethics course that is an elective, but hopefully can be moved to the core, which is at least two units. The students' response to it is absolutely overwhelming. The degree of inquiry, open-mindedness, and creative problem-solving is astounding. So I have noticed the shift from what the program had been earlier when most business schools had either no elective or compulsory ethical component. What I see happening in Berkeley from an evolutionary perspective is positive and I'm encouraged by it. The degree of creativity and open-mindedness among the undergraduate students is really heartening, especially with regard to attitudes toward the environment.

QUESTION: You encourage a "moderation and simplicity" model for us to use in addressing the massive environmental problems brought on by development and expansion. But isn't this approach lop-sided and even a bit disingenuous, as it favors the "over-developed" and privileged few who currently possess a near-monopoly on the world's goods and services? Doesn't it ignore the very real needs and desires of much of the developing world? What would you say to critics of this "less is more" approach who argue that only aggressive and widespread economic development and modernization can bring about social, political, and economic justice; a fair distribution of the world's resources? And that "moderation and simplicity" merely dooms most of humanity to lives of continuing impoverishment and backwardness? That it widens the gap between the "have" and "have-nots" and thus creates conditions that breed religious fundamentalism and terrorism?

TUCKER'S RESPONSE: This may be one of the most pressing problems facing us as a global community—how can we sustain life on the planet at the same time as providing an adequate standard of living for the growing human population which is now more than six billion people. Ever since the Rio Earth Summit of 1992 this has been a central focus of the United Nations efforts to promote "sustainable development," even though many have questioned the usefulness of the term itself. Indeed, the Rio summit was called the United Nations Conference on Environment and Development (UNCED) and brought together the largest number of heads of states ever gathered. In the last decade since UNCED, the United Nations has sponsored a series of international conferences to try and implement and expand Agenda 21, the major report that came out of the Rio conference. In September 2002 the United Nations sponsored another conference called the World Summit on Sustainable Development (WSSD) held in Johannesburg, South Africa.

All of these meetings and the ongoing work of the United Nations Development Programme (UNDP) and the United Nations Environment Programme (UNEP) represent a historic and unprecedented effort of the human community to find a way forward through the intractable maze of supporting economic development and preserving the environment on a global basis. The conflicts and the opportunities that have arisen around these issues in the United Nations and beyond may well define the shape of the twenty-first century. For it is quite true, as you suggest, that equitable distribution of the world's resources needs to be negotiated. Moreover, it is also true that many believe that development and modernization will bring greater benefits (economic, social, and political) to those in need. However, it is also the case that in the recent international meetings in Monterrey, Mexico, that optimistic position has been severely undermined by statistics that report that trade without aid is not working to promote development. In addition, the massive protests in recent years surrounding meetings of the World Trade Organization (WTO), the World Bank, the International Monetary Fund (IMF), and the G8 (countries representing the industrialized nations) has demonstrated significant disillusionment with free trade that ignores the environment, health, and fair labor practices.

I would suggest that in the midst of this difficult challenge of balancing the genuine need for appropriate development along with environmental preservation the religious community may discover a particularly important role. In other words, it is not a question of choosing between "justice" for the human and maintaining the "integrity of Creation" as some religions might phrase it. Rather, what is needed is to envision the conditions of a vibrant Earth community where the continuity of humans and the Earth is cherished and celebrated as a single multiform event. To give language to this realization may be the special task of the world's religions as they evoke the sensibilities and programs that are needed not simply for sustainable development but for sustainable life on the planet.

A specific document that provides a moral compass through the challenging path of sustainable development issues is the Earth Charter. This was first proposed as a soft law document at the Rio conference in 1992. However, it took five more years to bring this into being and to establish an Earth Council in Costa

Rica. At the Rio+5 conference in 1997 a Benchmark Draft was presented to the co-chairs Mikhail Gorbachev and Maurice Strong. The Earth Charter is based on a Preamble that outlines the cosmological context of our global situation and the challenges ahead. It states: "Humanity is part of a vast evolving universe. Earth, our home, is alive with a unique community of life. The forces of nature make existence a demanding and uncertain adventure, but Earth has provided the conditions essential to life's evolution." The Preamble concludes with a call that suggests we all share "responsibility for the present and future well-being of the human family and the larger living world. The spirit of human solidarity and kinship with all life is strengthened when we live with reverence for the mystery of being, gratitude for the gift of life, and humility regarding the human place in nature." It is in language such as this that the religious community can find resonance and a point of entry into these discussions on sustainability. For surely these qualities of reverence, gratitude, and humility are at the heart of our experience of both spirit and nature.

QUESTION: You described three concentric circles of expanding identity that we are situated within—the cosmological, historical, and religious. Moreover, you propose that the religious circle offers the best prospect for reinvigorating and enlarging our vision to unite us with this vast and interconnected universe. Yet what is it about religion *per se* that makes you optimistic? Hasn't organized religion more often served as a reactionary and regressive force, that shrinks our identity into narrow shards of clan, tribe, ethnic/national "us" versus "them"? Some would argue that religion, both in its scriptures and habits of exclusive claims, divides us not only from our fellow humans, but also fosters a hubris that sets us apart from and above nature itself. Karen Armstrong points out that religion at best is a two-faced god: one that heals and one that harms; that it often functions to insulate us from the very expansiveness you advocate; that it serves as a bulwark against change, the global, the loss of self. Isn't there another "circle" that lies beyond or within the religious that must be tapped? You allude to that in your Confucian quote. The religious impulse itself relies on something to inspire and continually rediscover this larger view. If so, what is it? And how do we nurture it often in opposition to religion itself?

TUCKER'S RESPONSE: This is a superb and thought-provoking question. I don't think, however, that I meant to suggest that the religious circle offers the *best* prospect for reinvigorating and enlarging our vision, but I would say it offers a viable and as yet not fully explored avenue for that task. In other words, there are many other paths to a reinvigorated vision. Nature writers in the United States such as Gary Snyder, Terry Tempest Williams, Barry Lopez, Scott Sanders, Richard Nelson, Pattiann Rogers and their predecessors such as Henry David Thoreau, John Muir, and Ralph Waldo Emerson provide such a gateway. They give the reader a fresh and unmediated sense of the power and mystery of the natural world. They evoke wonder, awe, mystery, fear, and gratitude in observing nature's many faces.

These are qualities of religious experience that you point toward when you observe that there is another circle within the religious one that needs to be tapped. It is true that there is something transreligious, if you will, about being in the presence of nature that needs to be evoked. That is in part what I was referring to with the idea of "worldly wonder." How does one become fully present to the elements, the soil, the plants, the flowers, the trees, and the winged, finned, scaled, and legged species that roam the planet? This requires entering into a space that can hold "intimate immensities" in creative equilibrium. It involves cultivating a multilayered sensibility of the deep interconnection of person, planet, and cosmos. It suggests that being in the presence of mystery is at the heart of the religious experience and this is what we sense in nature. No matter how much we know about its workings (and our sense of wonder can only be enhanced by scientific understanding) there is something that eludes us and yet attracts us beyond any words or means of expression. It is here in the ineffable silence that mystery makes itself felt and we are somehow transformed.

QUESTION: Can you speak at more length about how the "devaluation of matter" and the orientation toward a next world in many religious traditions may make it difficult for them to see the importance of the ecological crisis? Can you explore further some of the noumenon-in-phenomenon alternatives that you mention briefly (*Tathagatagarbha* doctrine, Creation Centered Spirituality) as possible guides for recognizing immanence in the natural world? Relatedly, what are we to do about the God-for-humans-only attitude of the Abrahamic religions if we want them to take responsibility for the fate of other species?

TUCKER'S RESPONSE: This other-worldly orientation that I referred to in my talk is indeed a major challenge for many of the world's religions with regard to activating environmental awareness and concern. However, it is not an insurmountable obstacle and it may be one of the ways in which the environmental crisis will also transform religions. Will religions simply watch the natural world being destroyed as passive witnesses awaiting salvation in the next world or will their sense of immanence be rekindled so as to respond in a timely manner to the current crisis? I think there are grounds for hope in the latter position.

The severe dichotomy of spirit and matter that has been a legacy of Enlightenment rationalism and of Cartesian dualism can no longer be sustained.

Indeed, the sciences of cosmology, quantum physics, and of evolutionary biology are giving us a highly sophisticated picture of the integrated nature of reality and of the self-organizing properties of matter itself. Emergent patterning and systems theory are pointing toward the deep integration of energy and matter.

Clearly matter can no longer be seen as dormant, dead, and disposable. The response of religious and non-religious people alike is one of an awakened sense of the wonder of life in its myriad material forms. From a wide variety of perspectives, then, from science and from religion, a new reverence and respect for the Earth is emerging.

Religions value matter from such perspectives as an indigenous recognition of a spirit presence in nature, such as *manitou* among the Anishinabe peoples in North America or the Shinto notion of *kami* (gods) referring to the presence of spirits in the natural world. The Chinese understanding of *qi* (translated as material force, vital force, and matter-energy) is that which infuses the entire universe. There are also expressions of the noumenon in the phenomenon such as in the Brahman-Atman (divine-self) identity of the Upanishadic tradition of Hinduism or the *Tathagatagarba* concept in Mahayana Buddhism where the Buddha Nature is present in all reality.

In the western religions the idea of creation *ex nihilo* by a Creator God grounds the importance of matter and Creation as a whole. Moreover, in Judaism *Shekinah* in the Kabbalistic tradition highlights the feminine presence of the divine in the natural world. In Christianity the doctrine of the Incarnation of Christ (the Word made flesh) and the understanding of the Cosmic Christ present in the universe are important bases for valuing matter. This is in part what has been emphasized by Creation Centered Spirituality developed by Matthew Fox and others who suggest that the world is the source of original blessing not of original sin. In Islam the Sufi term *wahdat al-wujud* refers to the unity of all being as manifest in the created order. These are all important counterpoints to a focus on God-human relations in the Abrahamic traditions or to an exclusive emphasis on otherworldly salvation as primary.

Epilogue

A MONTH BEFORE GIVING THE TALK *at the Graduate Theological Union I participated in a three-day international conference in Lyon, France co-chaired by Mikhail Gorbachev, now President of Green Cross International, and Maurice Strong, Chair of the Earth Council Foundation. It was titled "Earth Dialogues Forum" focusing on "Globalization and Sustainable Development: Is Ethics the Missing Link?" The United Nations Environment Programme was represented by its Director, Klaus Topfer, who underscored the importance of world religions regarding the environment, especially with respect to water issues. One of the unifying topics of discussion throughout the conference was the value of the Earth Charter as a document containing key principles for guiding sustainable development. As the moderator of the sessions for religious and spiritual leaders I addressed the final plenary session of the conference. These comments are adapted from that talk and will serve here as a conclusion that highlights the larger significance of the emerging dialogue of religion and ecology in international settings and in United Nations conferences addressing the challenge of a sustainable future.*

Plenary Address at Earth Dialogue Conference: Lyon, France February 23, 2002

*I*t is important to reflect on our times with a sense of realistic hope rather than with paralyzing despair.

We need to activate the possibilities of the necessary transformations that will ensure sustainable life and livelihood for future generations. History shows us that change is possible and that remarkable events are often sparked by the collective efforts of many people and by the steadfast leadership of numerous individuals. These efforts and those individuals are often unknown and yet they frequently make possible seemingly impossible transformations.

We are poised at such a historic moment when we are witnessing the European Union coming into economic integration along with political unification. Who would have imagined this was possible even half a century ago as Europe was recovering from two world wars? Similarly who could have predicted the collapse of the Berlin Wall and the end of the Cold War thanks to the leadership of Mikhail Gorbachev?

Who would have dreamed that the human community would begin to reimagine its destiny amidst signs of limits to unrestrained growth so as to redirect the course of human history toward a sustainable future? Who could imagine that the Earth Charter, a "Declaration of Interdependence," would now embody the ethical aspirations of the Earth community? And who could envision that the world's religions would be called to a new sense of mutual understanding and dialogue in their first great Parliament in 1893 in Chicago, and in the second Parliament in 1993 to assist in the creation of a Global Ethics?

If the European Union can model political and economic integration, if the great powers can withdraw from the Cold War, if the United Nations and the international community can point the way toward sustainable development, surely the religious communities can also become significant partners in identifying a compelling ethical vision for sustainable life on the planet. This is their challenge and ours. For they are called now to help us move from an exclusive preoccupation with Divine-human relations and even solely human-human relations to renewed human-Earth relations. From a concern for a human ethics regarding homicide, suicide, and genocide we are turning to a global ethics addressing biocide and geocide. This requires the voices of the spiritual traditions along with secular humanism.

This extension of ethics outward represents a major transformation for the world's religions from their theological and anthropological phase to their ecological and cosmological phase. And the Earth Charter embodies this great transformation in an extraordinarily comprehensive manner. For the human person is becoming decentered and recentered amidst the great concentric circles of life—from the individual and social circles to the circles of other species and ecosystems with which we share the web of life. And like the ripples in a pond, these circles move outward from the Earth to the universe itself. As the Earth Charter suggests in the Preamble, "Humanity is part of a vast evolving universe. Earth, our home, is alive with a unique community of life."

The religions have already known we are contained in the center of vast mysteries—we dwell amidst intimate immensities as the French philosopher, Gaston Bachelard, suggested. Historically the religions have shown us how to orient our lives set between hearth and cosmos. It is then the task of the religions to recover and recreate a language—both ecological and ethical—which reroots us in the Earth as our home.

For clearly the religions cannot stand by as silent witnesses to the sixth great extinction period which we inhabit or we too will join the endangered species list. Rather the human heart is waiting to participate in dialogue with the Earth. The human soul is poised to recover the language of the sacred that brings us back into contact with the great rhythms of the natural world. The religious traditions can help to unlock this language of dialogue with the Earth and for the Earth.

For buried deep within the symbol systems and ritual practices of the world's religions is a language of connection to the spiritual dimensions of nature itself. Life, death, rebirth, and renewal lie at the heart of both matter and spirit – at the core of both symbolic and biological realities. Religions, along with the great cultural traditions of art, music, dance, painting, poetry can lift up for us the voices of the Earth so that our dialogue will not be a monologue but a true conversation. With the help of our religious and cultural traditions a new kind of listening to the Earth is at hand, a new mode of hearing is now possible.

The call of the Earth is emerging; the cry of the species is sounding. The deep structural languages of the elements—air, water, soil, and fire—are becoming present to us. The call of the Earth is to see the Earth as the source of life not as a resource for our use alone. The cry of the species is for humans to join the great community of life forms not stand apart from it. The language of the elements reveals our inherent solidarity: air in our breath, soil in our bones, water in our blood, and fire in our hearts.

This call, these cries, this language reminds us that all religions have seen our body as part of the Earth body—that Earth is mother who has born us, nurtured us, and cared for us. And thus, as the world's religions suggest, our response to the Earth is one of continued gratitude for the gift of life. The religions remind us that at their heart is wonder and awe in the face of this mystery of existence, restraint and respect while partaking of its gifts, and a feeling of responsibility to future generations for its continuity.

As the religious voices emerge in concert with the voices of the Earth Community we will see once again that the common good is our common ground, that we are a late arrival amidst the vast evolution of the universe, but that our songs celebrating the extraordinary fecundity of life processes will point the way to renew the face of the Earth. Let the chorus begin.

PRESERVING AND CHERISHING THE EARTH: AN APPEAL FOR JOINT COMMITMENT IN SCIENCE AND RELIGION

Global Forum, Moscow
National Religious Partnership
for the Environment
January 1990

The Earth is the birthplace of our species and, so far as we know, our only home. When our numbers were small and our technology feeble, we were powerless to influence the environment of our world. But today, suddenly, almost without anyone noticing, our numbers have become immense; and our technology has achieved vast, even awesome, powers. Intentionally, or inadvertently, we are now able to make devastating changes in the global environment-an environment to which we and all the other beings with which we share the Earth are meticulously and exquisitely adapted.

We are now threatened by self-inflicted, swiftly moving environmental alterations about whose long-term biological and ecological consequences we are still painfully ignorant—depletion of the protective ozone layer; a global warming unprecedented in the last 150 millennia; the obliteration of an acre of forest every second; the rapid-fire extinction of species; and the prospect of a global nuclear war which would put at risk most of the population of the Earth. There may well be other such dangers of which, in our ignorance, we are still unaware. Individually and cumulatively they represent a trap being set for the human species, a trap we are setting for ourselves. However principled and lofty (or naïve and shortsighted) the justifications may have been for the activities that brought forth these dangers, separately and together they now imperil our species and many others. We are close to committing-many would argue we are already committing-what in religious language is sometimes called Crimes against Creation.

By their very nature these assaults on the environment were not caused by one political group or any one generation. Intrinsically, they are transnational, transgenerational, and transideological. So are all conceivable solutions. To escape these traps requires a perspective that embraces the peoples of the planet and all the generations yet to come.

Problems of such magnitude, and solutions demanding so broad a perspective must be recognized from the outset as having a religious as well as a scientific dimension. Mindful of our common responsibility, we scientists-many of us long engaged in combating the environmental crisis-urgently appeal to the world religious community to commit, in word and deed, and as boldly as is required, to preserve the environment of the Earth.

Some of the short-term mitigations of these dangers—such as greater energy efficiency, rapid banning of chlorofluorocarbons, or modest reductions in the nuclear arsenals—are comparatively easy and at some level are already under way. But other, more far-reaching, more long-term, more effective approaches will encounter widespread inertia, denial, and resistance. In this category are conversion from fossil fuels to a nonpolluting energy economy, a continuing swift reversal of the nuclear arms race, and a voluntary halt to world population growth—

without which many of the other approaches to preserve the environment will be nullified.

As on issues of peace, human rights, and social justice, religious institutions can here too be a strong force encouraging national and international initiatives in both the private and public sectors, and in the diverse worlds of commerce, education, culture, and mass communication.

The environmental crisis requires radical changes not only in public policy, but in individual behavior. The historical record makes clear that religious teaching, example, and leadership are powerfully able to influence personal conduct and commitment.

As scientists, many of us have had profound experiences of awe and reverence before the universe. We understand that what is regarded as sacred is more likely to be treated with care and respect. Our planetary home should be so regarded. Efforts to safeguard and cherish the environment need to be infused with a vision of the sacred. At the same time, a much wider and deeper understanding of science and technology is needed. If we do not understand the problem, it is unlikely we will be able to fix it. Thus, there is a vital role for religion and science.

We know that the well-being of our planetary environment is already a source of profound concern in your councils and congregations. We hope this Appeal will encourage a sprit of common cause and joint action to help preserve the Earth.

List of Signatories*

CARL SAGAN
Cornell University, Ithaca, New York

---

*Affiliations are given for identification purposes only.

HANS A. BETHE
Cornell University, Ithaca, New York

S. CHANDRASEKHAR
University of Chicago, Chicago, Illinois

PAUL J. CRUTZEN
Max Planck Institute for Chemistry, Mainz, West
Germany

FREEMAN J. DYSON
Institute for Advanced Study, Princeton, New Jersey

RICHARD L. GARWIN
IBM Corporation, Yorktown Heights, New York

STEPHEN JAY GOULD
Harvard University, Cambridge, Massachusetts

JAMES HANSEN
NASA Goddard Institute for Space Studies, New York,
New York

MOHAMMED KASSAS
University of Cairo, Cairo, Egypt

MOTOO KIMURA
National Institute of Genetics, Mishima, Japan

THOMAS MALONE
St. Joseph College, West Hartford, Connecticut

PETER RAVEN
Missouri Botanical Garden, St. Louis, Missouri

ROGER REVELLE
University of California San Diego, La Jolla, California

WALTER ORR
Roberts National Center for Atmospheric Research,
Boulder, Colorado

ABDUS SALAM
International Centre for Theoretical Physics, Trieste,
Italy

STEPHEN H. SCHNEIDER
National Center for Atmospheric Research, Boulder,
Colorado

HANS SUESS
University of California San Diego, La Jolla, California

O.B. TOOM
NASA Ames Research Center, Moffett Field, California

RICHARD P. TURCO
University of California, Los Angeles, California

SIR FREDERICK WARNER
Essex University, Colchester, United Kingdom

VICTOR F. WEISSKOPF
Massachusetts Institute of Technology, Cambridge,
Massachusetts

JEROME B. WIESNER
Massachusetts Institute of Technology, Cambridge,
Massachusetts

ROBERT R. WILSON
Cornell University, Ithaca, New York

THE JOINT APPEAL IN RELIGION AND SCIENCE: STATEMENT BY RELIGIOUS LEADERS AT THE SUMMIT ON ENVIRONMENT

June 3, 1991
New York City

NATIONAL RELIGIOUS PARTNERSHIP FOR THE ENVIRONMENT

HISTORICAL NOTE

The Summit on Environment, sponsored by the Joint Appeal in Religion and Science, grew out of a collaboration which began in January 1990 with an Open Letter to the Religious Community sent by 34 internationally renowned scientists. Of the peril to planetary environment they wrote: "Problems of such magnitude and solutions demanding so broad a perspective must be recognized from the outset as having a religious as well as a scientific dimension . . . Efforts to safeguard and cherish the environment need to be infused with a vision of the sacred."

Struck by the initiative, several hundred religious leaders of all major faiths from all five continents responded: "This invitation to collaboration marks a unique moment and opportunity in the relationship of science and religion. We are eager to explore, as soon as possible, concrete, specific forms of action."

The Summit on Environment was held on June 2nd and 3rd, 1991, at the American Museum of Natural History and the Cathedral of St. John the Divine. It was a next step in an ongoing partnership and an effort to support the American religious community as it moves forward to act upon the vision of environmental justice and sustainable future.

On a spring evening and the following day in New York City, we representatives of the religious community in the United States of America gathered to deliberate and plan action in response to the crisis of the Earth's environment.

Deep impulses brought us together. Almost daily, we note mounting evidence of environmental destruction and ever-increasing peril to life, whole species, whole ecosystems. Many people, and particularly the young, want to know where we stand and what we intend to do. And, finally, it is what God made and beheld as good that is under assault. The future of this gift so freely given is in our hands, and we must maintain it as we have received it. This is an inescapably religious challenge. We feel a profound and urgent call to respond with all we have, all we are, and all we believe.

We chose to meet, these two days, in the company of people from diverse traditions and disciplines. No one perspective alone is equal to the crisis we face-spiritual and moral, economic and cultural, institutional and personal. For our part, we were grateful to strengthen a collaboration with distinguished scientists and to take stock of their testimony on problems besetting planetary ecology. As people of faith, we were also moved by the support for our work from distinguished public policy leaders.

What we heard left us more troubled than ever. Global warming, generated mainly by the burning of fossil fuels and deforestation, is widely predicted to increase temperatures worldwide, changing climate patterns, increasing drought in many areas, threatening agriculture, wildlife, the integrity of natural ecosystems and creating millions of environmental refugees. Depletion of the ozone shield, caused by human-made chemical agents such as chlorofluorocarbons, lets in deadly ultraviolet radiation from the Sun, with predicted consequences that include skin cancer, cataracts, damage to the human immune system, and destruction of the primary photosynthetic producers at the base of the food chain on which other life depends. Our expanding technological civilization is destroying an acre and a half of forest every second. The accelerating loss of species of plants, animals, and microorganisms which threatens the irreversible loss of up to a fifth of the total number within the next thirty years, is not only morally reprehensible but is increasingly limiting the prospects for sustainable productivity. No effort, however heroic, to deal with these global conditions and the interrelated issues of social justice can succeed unless we address the increasing population of the Earth-especially the billion poorest people who have every right to expect a decent standard of living. So too, we must find ways to reduce the disproportionate consumption of natural resources by affluent industrial societies like ours.

Much would tempt us to deny or push aside this global environmental crisis and refuse even to consider the fundamental changes of human behavior required to address it. *But we religious leaders accept a prophetic responsibility to make known the full dimensions of this challenge, and what is required to address it, to the many millions we reach, teach, and counsel.*

We intend to be informed participants in discussions of these issues and to contribute our views on the moral and ethical imperative for developing national and international policy responses. But we declare here and now that steps must be taken toward: accelerated phaseout of ozone depleting chemicals; much more efficient use of fossil fuels and the development of a non-fossil fuel economy; preservation of tropical forests and other measures to protect continued biological diversity; and concerted efforts to slow the dramatic and dangerous growth in world population through empowering both women and men, encouraging economic self-sufficiency, and making family planning services available to all who may consider them on a strictly voluntary basis.

We believe a consensus now exists, at the highest level of leadership across a significant spectrum of religious traditions, that the cause of environmental integrity and justice must occupy a position of utmost priority for people of faith. Response to this issue can and must cross traditional religious and political lines. It has the potential to unify and renew religious life.

We pledge to take the initiative in interpreting and communicating theological foundations for the stewardship of Creation in which we find the principles for environmental action. Here our seminaries have a critical role to play. So too, there is a call for moral transformation, as we recognize that the roots of environmental destruction lie in human pride, greed, and selfishness, as well as the appeal of the short-term over the long-term.

We reaffirm here, in the strongest possible terms, the indivisibility of social justice and ecological integrity. An equitable international economic order is essential for preserving the global environment. Economic equity, racial justice, gender equality, and environmental well-being are interconnected and all are essential to peace. To help ensure these, we pledge to mobilize public opinion and to appeal to elected officials and leaders in the private sector. In our congregations and corporate life, we will encourage and seek to exemplify habits of sound and sustainable householding-

in land use, investment decisions, energy conservation, purchasing of products, and waste disposal.

Commitments to these areas of action we pledged to one another solemnly and in a spirit of mutual accountability. We dare not let our resolve falter. We will continue to work together, add to our numbers, and deepen our collaboration with the worlds of science and government. We also agreed this day to the following initiatives:

1. We will widely distribute this declaration within the religious community and beyond. We have established a continuing mechanism to coordinate ongoing activities among us, working intimately with existing program and staff resources in the religious world. We will reach out to other leaders across the broadest possible spectrum of religious life. We will help organize other such gatherings as ours within individual faith groups, in interfaith and interdisciplinary formats, and at international, national, and regional levels.

2. We religious leaders and members of the scientific community will call together a Washington D.C. convocation and meet with members of the Executive and Congressional branches to express our support for bold steps on behalf of environmental integrity and justice. There too we will consider ways to facilitate legislative testimony by religious leaders and response to local environmental action alerts.

3. We will witness first-hand and call public attention to the effect of environmental degradation on vulnerable peoples and ecosystems.

4. We will call a meeting of seminary deans and faculty to review and initiate curriculum development and promote

bibliographies emphasizing stewardship of Creation. We will seek ways to establish internships for seminarians in organizations working on the environment and for young scientists in the study of social ethics.

5. We will prepare educational materials for congregations, provide technical support for religious publishers already producing such materials, and share sermonical and liturgical materials about ecology.

6. We will establish an instrument to help place stories on environment in faith group and denominational newsletters and help assure coverage of the religious community's environmental activities in the secular press.

7. We will urge compliance with the Valdez Principles and preach and promote corporate responsibility.

8. We will encourage establishment of one model environmentally sound and sustainable facility within each faith group and denomination. We will provide materials for environmental audits and facilitate bulk purchasing of environmentally sound products.

It has taken the religious community, as others, much time and reflection to start to comprehend the full scale and nature of this crisis and even to glimpse what it will require of us. We must pray ceaselessly for wisdom, courage, and creativity. Most importantly, we are people of faith and hope. These qualities are what we may most uniquely have to offer to this effort. We pledge to the children of the world and, in the words of the Iroquois, "to the seventh generation," that we will take full measure of what this moment in history requires of us. In this challenge may lie the opportunity for people of faith to affirm and enact, at a scale such as never before, what it truly means to be religious. And so we have begun, believing there can be no turning back.

List of Signatories*

BISHOP VINTON R. ANDERSON
President, World Council of Churches

RABBI MARC D. ANGEL
President, Rabbinical Council of America

THE MOST REVEREND EDMOND L. BROWNING
Presiding Bishop and Primate of the Episcopal Church

REVEREND JOAN CAMPBELL
General-Secretary, National Council of Churches of Christ

REVEREND HERBERT W. CHILSTROM
Bishop, Evangelical Lutheran Church in America

FATHER DREW CHRISTIANSEN, S.J.
Director, Office of International Justice and Peace, United States Catholic Conference

MS. BEVERLY DAVISON
President, American Baptist Church

REVEREND DR. MILTON B. EFTHIMIOU
Director of Church and Society Greek Orthodox Archdioceses of North and South America

BISHOP WILLIAM B. FRIEND
Chairman of the Committee for Science and Human Values, National Conference of Catholic Bishops

*Affiliations for identification purposes only.

DR. ALFRED GOTTSCHALK
President, Hebrew Union College, Jewish Institute of Religion

DR. ARTHUR GREEN
President, Reconstructionist Rabbinical College

HIS EMINENCE ARCHBISHOP IAKOVOS
Primate, Greek Orthodox Archdiocese of North and South America

WORLD SCIENTISTS' WARNINGS TO HUMANITY

Union of Concerned Scientists

This 1992 document was signed by 1,575 of the world's most prominent scientists (including 99 of the 196 living Nobel laureates) and was sent to governmental leaders all over the world. The document asks people to take immediate action to stop the ever-increasing environmental degradation that threatens global life support systems on this planet. The appeal was coordinated by Dr. Henry Kendall, Nobel laureate (1990, Physics), and former Chairperson of the Union of Concerned Scientists.

WORLD SCIENTISTS' WARNING TO HUMANITY

INTRODUCTION

Human beings and the natural world are on a collision course. Human activities inflict harsh and often irreversible damage on the environment and on critical resources. If not checked, many of our current practices put at serious risk the future that we wish for human society and the plant and animal kingdoms, and may so alter the living world that it will be unable to sustain life in the manner that we know. Fundamental changes are urgent if we are to avoid the collision our present course will bring about.

THE ENVIRONMENT

The environment is suffering critical stress:

THE ATMOSPHERE

Stratospheric ozone depletion threatens us with enhanced ultra-violet radiation at the earth's surface, which can be damaging or lethal to many life forms. Air pollution near ground level, and acid precipitation, are already causing widespread injury to humans, forests, and crops.

WATER RESOURCES

Heedless exploitation of depletable ground water supplies endangers food production and other essential human systems. Heavy demands on the world's surface waters have resulted in serious shortages in some 80 countries, containing 40 percent of the world's population. Pollution of rivers, lakes, and ground water further limits the supply.

OCEANS

Destructive presure on the oceans is severe, particularly in the coastal regions which produce most of the world's food fish. The total marine catch is now at or above the estimated maximum sustainable yield. Some fisheries have already shown signs of collapse. Rivers carrying heavy burdens of eroded soil into the seas also carry industrial, municipal, agricultural, and livestock waste—some of it toxic.

SOIL

Loss of soil productivity, which is causing extensive land abandonment, is a widespread byproduct of current practices in agriculture and animal husbandry. Since 1945, 11 percent of the earth's vegetated surface has been degraded—an area larger than India and China combined—and per capita food production in many parts of the world is decreasing.

FORESTS

Tropical rain forests, as well as tropical and temperate dry forests, are being destroyed rapidly. At present rates, some critical forest types will be gone in a few years, and most of the tropical rain forest will be gone before the end of the next century. With them will go large numbers of plant and animal species.

LIVING SPECIES

The irreversible loss of species, which by 2100 may reach one third of all species now living, is especially serious. We are losing the potential they hold for providing medicinal and other benefits, and the contribution that genetic diversity of life forms gives to the robustness of the world's biological systems and to the astonishing beauty of the earth itself.

Much of this damage is irreversible on a scale of centuries or permanent. Other processes appear to pose additional threats. Increasing levels of gases in the atmosphere from human activities, including carbon dioxide released from fossil fuel burning and from deforestation, may alter climate on a global scale. Predictions of global warming are still uncertain—with projected effects ranging from tolerable to very severe—but potential risks are very great.

Our massive tampering with the world's interdependent web of life—coupled with the environmental damage inflicted by deforestation, species loss, and climate change—could trigger widespread adverse effects, including unpredictable collapses of critical biological systems whose interactions and dynamics we only imperfectly understand.

Uncertainty over the extent of these effects cannot excuse complacency or delay in facing the threats.

POPULATION

The earth is finite. Its ability to absorb wastes and destructive effluent is finite. Its ability to provide food and energy is finite. Its ability to provide for growing numbers of people is finite. And we are fast approaching many of the earth's limits. Current economic practices which damage the environment, in both developed and underdeveloped nations, cannot be continued without the risk that vital global systems will be damaged beyond repair.

Pressures resulting from unrestrained population growth put demands on the natural world that can overwhelm any efforts to achieve a sustainable future. If we are to halt the destruction of our environment, we must accept limits to that growth. A World Bank estimate indicates that world population will not stabilize at less than 12.4 billion, while the United Nations concludes that the eventual total could reach 14 billion, a near tripling of today's 5.4 billion. But, even at this moment, one person in five lives in absolute poverty without enough to eat, and one in ten suffers serious malnutrition.

No more than one or a few decades remain before the chance to avert the threats we now confront will be lost and the prospects for humanity immeasurably diminished.

WARNING

We the undersigned, senior members of the world's scientific community, hereby warn all humanity of what lies ahead. A great change in our stewardship of the earth and the life on it, is required, if vast human misery is to be avoided and our global home on this planet is not to be irretrievably mutilated.

WHAT WE MUST DO

Five inextricably linked areas must be addressed simultaneously:

1. We must bring environmentally damaging activities under control to restore and protect the integrity of the earth's systems we depend on.

We must, for example, move away from fossil fuels to more benign, inexhaustible energy sources to cut greenhouse gas emissions and the pollution of our air and water. Priority must be give to the development of energy sources matched to third world needs—small scale and relatively easy to implement.
We must halt deforestation, injury to and loss of agricultural land, and the loss of terrestrial and marine plant and animal species.

2. We must manage resources crucial to human welfare more effectively.

We must give high priority to efficient use of energy, water, and other materials, including expansion of conservation and recycling.

3. We must stabilize population. This will be possible only if all nations recognize that it requires improved social and economic conditions, and the adoption of effective, voluntary family planning.

4. We must reduce and eventually eliminate poverty.

5. We must ensure sexual equality, and guarantee women control over their own reproductive decisions.

The developed nations are the largest polluters in the world today. They must greatly reduce their overconsumption, if we are to reduce pressures on resources and the global environment. The developed nations have the obligation to provide aid and support to developing nations, because only the developed nations have the financial resources and the technical skills for these tasks.

Acting on this recognition is not altruism, but enlightened self-interest: whether industrialized or not, we all have but one lifeboat. No nation can escape from injury when global biological systems are damaged. No nation can escape from conflicts over increasingly scarce resources. In addition, environmental and economic instabilities will cause mass migrations with incalculable consequences for developed and undeveloped nations alike.

Developing nations must realize that environmental damage is one of the gravest threats they face, and that attempts to blunt it will be overwhelmed if their populations go unchecked. The greatest peril is to become trapped in spirals of environmental decline, poverty, and unrest, leading to social, economic, and environmental collapse.

Success in this global endeavor will require a great reduction in violence and war. Resources now devoted to the preparation and conduct of war—amounting to over $1 trillion annually—will be badly needed in the new tasks and should be diverted to the new challenges.

A new ethic is required—a new attitude toward discharging our responsibility for caring for ourselves and for the earth. We must recognize the earth's limited capacity to provide for us. We must recognize its fragility. We must no longer allow it to be ravaged. This ethic must motivate a great movement, convincing reluctant leaders and reluctant governments and reluctant peoples themselves to effect the needed changes.

The scientists issuing this warning hope that our message will reach and affect people everywhere. We need the help of many.

We require the help of the world community of scientists—natural, social, economic, political;

We require the help of the world's business and industrial leaders;

We require the help of the world's religious leaders; and

We require the help of the world's peoples.

We call on all to join us in this task.

THE EARTH CHARTER

APPENDIX IV

Background:

In 1987 the United Nations World Commission on
Environment and Development issued a call for creation of
a new charter that would set forth fundamental principles
for sustainable development. The drafting of an Earth
Charter was part of the unfinished business of the 1992
Rio Earth Summit. In 1994 Maurice Strong, the secretary
general of the Earth Summit and chairman of the Earth
Council, and Mikhail Gorbachev, president of Green Cross
International launched a new Earth Charter initiative with
support from the Dutch government.

An Earth Charter Commission was formed in 1997 to
oversee the project and an Earth Charter Secretariat was
established in Costa Rica. Early in 1997, the Earth Charter
Commission formed an international drafting committee.
Beginning with the Benchmark Draft issued by the
Commission following the Rio+5 Forum in Rio de Janeiro
drafts were circulated internationally as part of the
consultation process. Meeting in UNESCO Headquarters in
Paris in March 2000 the Commission approved the final
version of the Earth Charter.

The Earth Charter is the product of a decade long,
worldwide, cross-cultural conversation about common goals
and shard values. The drafting of the Earth Charter has
involved the most open and participatory consultation
process ever conducted in connection with an international
document.

For more on the Earth Charter Initiative see
www.earthcharter.org

PREAMBLE

We stand at a critical moment in Earth's history, a time
when humanity must choose its future. As the world
becomes increasingly interdependent and fragile, the future
at once holds great peril and great promise. To move forward
we must recognize that in the midst of a magnificent
diversity of cultures and life forms we are one human family
and one Earth community with a common destiny. We
must join together to bring forth a sustainable global society
founded on respect for nature, universal human rights,
economic justice, and a culture of peace. Towards this end,
it is imperative that we, the peoples of Earth, declare our
responsibility to one another, to the greater community of
life, and to future generations.

EARTH, OUR HOME

Humanity is part of a vast evolving universe. Earth, our
home, is alive with a unique community of life. The forces
of nature make existence a demanding and uncertain
adventure, but Earth has provided the conditions essential
to life's evolution. The resilience of the community of life
and the well-being of humanity depend upon preserving a
healthy biosphere with all its ecological systems, a rich
variety of plants and animals, fertile soils, pure waters, and
clean air. The global environment with its finite resources is
a common concern of all peoples. The protection of Earth's
vitality, diversity, and beauty is a sacred trust.

THE GLOBAL SITUATION

The dominant patterns of production and consumption
are causing environmental devastation, the depletion of

resources, and a massive extinction of species. Communities are being undermined. The benefits of development are not shared equitably and the gap between rich and poor is widening. Injustice, poverty, ignorance, and violent conflict are widespread and the cause of great suffering. An unprecedented rise in human population has overburdened ecological and social systems. The foundations of global security are threatened. These trends are perilous—but not inevitable.

THE CHALLENGES AHEAD

The choice is ours: form a global partnership to care for Earth and one another or risk the destruction of ourselves and the diversity of life. Fundamental changes are needed in our values, institutions, and ways of living. We must realize that when basic needs have been met, human development is primarily about being more, not having more. We have the knowledge and technology to provide for all and to reduce our impacts on the environment. The emergence of a global civil society is creating new opportunities to build a democratic and humane world. Our environmental, economic, political, social, and spiritual challenges are interconnected, and together we can forge inclusive solutions.

UNIVERSAL RESPONSIBILITY

To realize these aspirations, we must decide to live with a sense of universal responsibility, identifying ourselves with the whole Earth community as well as our local communities. We are at once citizens of different nations and of one world in which the local and global are linked. Everyone shares responsibility for the present and future well-being of the human family and the larger living world. The spirit of human solidarity and kinship with all life is strengthened when we live with reverence for the mystery of being, gratitude for the gift of life, and humility regarding the human place in nature.

We urgently need a shared vision of basic values to provide an ethical foundation for the emerging world community. Therefore, together in hope we affirm the following interdependent principles for a sustainable way of life as a common standard by which the conduct of all individuals, organizations, businesses, governments, and transnational institutions is to be guided and assessed.

PRINCIPLES

I. RESPECT AND CARE FOR THE COMMUNITY OF LIFE

1. Respect Earth and life in all its diversity.
    a. Recognize that all beings are interdependent and every form of life has value regardless of its worth to human beings.
    b. Affirm faith in the inherent dignity of all human beings and in the intellectual, artistic, ethical, and spiritual potential of humanity.
2. Care for the community of life with understanding, compassion, and love.
    a. Accept that with the right to own, manage, and use natural resources comes the duty to prevent environmental harm and to protect the rights of people.
    b. Affirm that with increased freedom, knowledge, and power comes increased responsibility to promote the common good.

3. Build democratic societies that are just, participatory, sustainable, and peaceful.
   a. Ensure that communities at all levels guarantee human rights and fundamental freedoms and provide everyone an opportunity to realize his or her full potential.
   b. Promote social and economic justice, enabling all to achieve a secure and meaningful livelihood that is ecologically responsible.
4. Secure Earth's bounty and beauty for present and future generations.
   a. Recognize that the freedom of action of each generation is qualified by the needs of future generations.
   b. Transmit to future generations values, traditions, and institutions that support the long-term flourishing of Earth's human and ecological communities.

In order to fulfill these four broad commitments, it is necessary to:

II. ECOLOGICAL INTEGRITY

5. Protect and restore the integrity of Earth's ecological systems, with special concern for biological diversity and the natural processes that sustain life.
   a. Adopt at all levels sustainable development plans and regulations that make environmental conservation and rehabilitation integral to all development initiatives.
   b. Establish and safeguard viable nature and biosphere reserves, including wild lands and marine areas, to protect Earth's life support systems, maintain biodiversity, and preserve our natural heritage.

    c.   Promote the recovery of endangered species and ecosystems.

    d.   Control and eradicate non-native or genetically modified organisms harmful to native species and the environment, and prevent introduction of such harmful organisms.

    e.   Manage the use of renewable resources such as water, soil, forest products, and marine life in ways that do not exceed rates of regeneration and that protect the health of ecosystems.

    f.   Manage the extraction and use of non-renewable resources such as minerals and fossil fuels in ways that minimize depletion and cause no serious environmental damage.

6.   Prevent harm as the best method of environmental protection and, when knowledge is limited, apply a precautionary approach.

    a.   Take action to avoid the possibility of serious or irreversible environmental harm even when scientific knowledge is incomplete or inconclusive.

    b.   Place the burden of proof on those who argue that a proposed activity will not cause significant harm, and make the responsible parties liable for environmental harm.

    c.   Ensure that decision making addresses the cumulative, long-term, indirect, long distance, and global consequences of human activities.

    d.   Prevent pollution of any part of the environment and allow no build-up of radioactive, toxic, or other hazardous substances.

    e.   Avoid military activities damaging to the environment.

7.   Adopt patterns of production, consumption, and reproduction that safeguard Earth's regenerative capacities, human rights, and community well-being.

a. Reduce, reuse, and recycle the materials used in production and consumption systems, and ensure that residual waste can be assimilated by ecological systems.

b. Act with restraint and efficiency when using energy, and rely increasingly on renewable energy sources such as solar and wind.

c. Promote the development, adoption, and equitable transfer of environmentally sound technologies.

d. Internalize the full environmental and social costs of goods and services in the selling price, and enable consumers to identify products that meet the highest social and environmental standards.

e. Ensure universal access to health care that fosters reproductive health and responsible reproduction.

f. Adopt lifestyles that emphasize the quality of life and material sufficiency in a finite world.

8. Advance the study of ecological sustainability and promote the open exchange and wide application of the knowledge acquired.

a. Support international scientific and technical cooperation on sustainability, with special attention to the needs of developing nations.

b. Recognize and preserve the traditional knowledge and spiritual wisdom in all cultures that contribute to environmental protection and human well-being.

c. Ensure that information of vital importance to human health and environmental protection, including genetic information, remains available in the public domain.

III. SOCIAL AND ECONOMIC JUSTICE

9. Eradicate poverty as an ethical, social, and environmental imperative.
   a. Guarantee the right to potable water, clean air, food security, uncontaminated soil, shelter, and safe sanitation, allocating the national and international resources required.
   b. Empower every human being with the education and resources to secure a sustainable livelihood, and provide social security and safety nets for those who are unable to support themselves.
   c. Recognize the ignored, protect the vulnerable, serve those who suffer, and enable them to develop their capacities and to pursue their aspirations.
10. Ensure that economic activities and institutions at all levels promote human development in an equitable and sustainable manner.
    a. Promote the equitable distribution of wealth within nations and among nations.
    b. Enhance the intellectual, financial, technical, and social resources of developing nations, and relieve them of onerous international debt.
    c. Ensure that all trade supports sustainable resource use, environmental protection, and progressive labor standards.
    d. Require multinational corporations and international financial organizations to act transparently in the public good, and hold them accountable for the consequences of their activities.
11. Affirm gender equality and equity as prerequisites to sustainable development and ensure universal access to education, health care, and economic opportunity.

a. Secure the human rights of women and girls and end all violence against them.

b. Promote the active participation of women in all aspects of economic, political, civil, social, and cultural life as full and equal partners, decision makers, leaders, and beneficiaries.

c. Strengthen families and ensure the safety and loving nurture of all family members.

12. Uphold the right of all, without discrimination, to a natural and social environment supportive of human dignity, bodily health, and spiritual well-being, with special attention to the rights of indigenous peoples and minorities.

a. Eliminate discrimination in all its forms, such as that based on race, color, sex, sexual orientation, religion, language, and national, ethnic or social origin.

b. Affirm the right of indigenous peoples to their spirituality, knowledge, lands and resources and to their related practice of sustainable livelihoods.

c. Honor and support the young people of our communities, enabling them to fulfill their essential role in creating sustainable societies.

d. Protect and restore outstanding places of cultural and spiritual significance.

IV. DEMOCRACY, NONVIOLENCE, AND PEACE

13. Strengthen democratic institutions at all levels, and provide transparency and accountability in governance, inclusive participation in decision making, and access to justice.

a. Uphold the right of everyone to receive clear and timely information on environmental matters and all development plans and activities which are likely to affect them or in which they have an interest.

b. Support local, regional and global civil society, and promote the meaningful participation of all interested individuals and organizations in decision making.

c. Protect the rights to freedom of opinion, expression, peaceful assembly, association, and dissent.

d. Institute effective and efficient access to administrative and independent judicial procedures, including remedies and redress for environmental harm and the threat of such harm.

e. Eliminate corruption in all public and private institutions.

f. Strengthen local communities, enabling them to care for their environments, and assign environmental responsibilities to the levels of government where they can be carried out most effectively.

14. Integrate into formal education and life-long learning the knowledge, values, and skills needed for a sustainable way of life.

a. Provide all, especially children and youth, with educational opportunities that empower them to contribute actively to sustainable development.

b. Promote the contribution of the arts and humanities as well as the sciences in sustainability education.

c. Enhance the role of the mass media in raising awareness of ecological and social challenges.

d. Recognize the importance of moral and spiritual education for sustainable living.

15. Treat all living beings with respect and consideration.

a. Prevent cruelty to animals kept in human societies and protect them from suffering.

b. Protect wild animals from methods of hunting, trapping, and fishing that cause extreme, prolonged, or avoidable suffering.

c. Avoid or eliminate to the full extent possible the taking or destruction of non-targeted species.

16. Promote a culture of tolerance, nonviolence, and peace.

a. Encourage and support mutual understanding, solidarity, and cooperation among all peoples and within and among nations.

b. Implement comprehensive strategies to prevent violent conflict and use collaborative problem solving to manage and resolve environmental conflicts and other disputes.

c. Demilitarize national security systems to the level of a non-provocative defense posture, and convert military resources to peaceful purposes, including ecological restoration.

d. Eliminate nuclear, biological, and toxic weapons and other weapons of mass destruction.

e. Ensure that the use of orbital and outer space supports environmental protection and peace.

f. Recognize that peace is the wholeness created by right relationships with oneself, other persons, other cultures, other life, Earth, and the larger whole of which all are a part.

THE WAY FORWARD

As never before in history, common destiny beckons us to seek a new beginning. Such renewal is the promise of these Earth Charter principles. To fulfill this promise, we must commit ourselves to adopt and promote the values and objectives of the Charter.

This requires a change of mind and heart. It requires a new sense of global interdependence and universal responsibility. We must imaginatively develop and apply the vision of a sustainable way of life locally, nationally, regionally, and globally. Our cultural diversity is a precious heritage and different cultures will find their own distinctive ways to realize the vision. We must deepen and expand the global dialogue that generated the Earth Charter, for we have much to learn from the ongoing collaborative search for truth and wisdom.

Life often involves tensions between important values. This can mean difficult choices. However, we must find ways to harmonize diversity with unity, the exercise of freedom with the common good, short-term objectives with long-term goals. Every individual, family, organization, and community has a vital role to play. The arts, sciences, religions, educational institutions, media, businesses, nongovernmental organizations, and governments are all called to offer creative leadership. The partnership of government, civil society, and business is essential for effective governance.

In order to build a sustainable global community, the nations of the world must renew their commitment to the United Nations, fulfill their obligations under existing international agreements, and support the implementation of Earth Charter principles with an international legally binding instrument on environment and development.

Let ours be a time remembered for the awakening of a new reverence for life, the firm resolve to achieve sustainability, the quickening of the struggle for justice and peace, and the joyful celebration of life.

COMMON DECLARATION BY POPE JOHN PAUL II AND ECUMENICAL PATRIARCH BARTHOLOMEW I

June 10, 2002
Venice, Italy

ROMAN CATHOLIC-EASTERN ORTHODOX
JOINT DECLARATION ON THE ENVIRONMENT,
SIGNED BY POPE JOHN PAUL II AND
PATRIARCH BARTHOLOMEW I OF
CONSTANTINOPLE

"WE ARE STILL BETRAYING THE MANDATE GOD HAS GIVEN US"

We are gathered here today in the spirit of peace for the good of all human beings and for the care of creation. At this moment in history, at the beginning of the third millennium, we are saddened to see the daily suffering of a great number of people from violence, starvation, poverty, and disease.

We are also concerned about the negative consequences for humanity and for all creation resulting from the degradation of some basic natural resources such as water, air and land, brought about by an economic and technological progress which does not recognize and take into account its limits.

Almighty God envisioned a world of beauty and harmony, and He created it, making every part an expression of His freedom, wisdom and love (cf. Genesis 1:1–25).

At the center of the whole of creation, He placed us, human beings, with our inalienable human dignity. Although we share many features with the rest of the living beings, Almighty God went further with us and gave us an immortal soul, the source of self-awareness and freedom, endowments that make us in His image and likeness (cf. Gen. 1:26–31; 2:7). Marked with that resemblance, we have been placed by God in the world in order to cooperate with Him in realizing more and more fully the divine purpose for creation.

At the beginning of history, man and woman sinned by disobeying God and rejecting His design for creation. Among the results of this first sin was the destruction of the original harmony of creation. If we examine carefully the social and environmental crisis which the world community is facing, we must conclude that we are still betraying the mandate God has given us: to be stewards called to collaborate with God in watching over creation in holiness and wisdom.

God has not abandoned the world. It is His will that His design and our hope for it will be realized through our co-operation in restoring its original harmony. In our own time we are witnessing a growth of an ecological awareness which needs to be encouraged, so that it will lead to practical programs and initiatives. An awareness of the relationship between God and humankind brings a fuller sense of the importance of the relationship between human beings and the natural environment, which is God's creation and which God entrusted to us to guard with wisdom and love (cf. Gen. 1:28).

Respect for creation stems from respect for human life and dignity. It is on the basis of our recognition that the world is created by God that we can discern an objective moral order within which to articulate a code of environmental ethics. In this perspective, Christians and all other believers have a specific role to play in proclaiming moral values and in educating people in ecological awareness, which is none other than responsibility towards self, towards others, towards creation.

What is required is an act of repentance on our part and a renewed attempt to view ourselves, one another, and the world around us within the perspective of the divine design for creation. The problem is not simply economic and technological; it is moral and spiritual. A solution at the economic and technological level can be found only if we undergo, in the most radical way, an inner change of heart, which can lead to a change in lifestyle and of unsustainable patterns of consumption and production. A genuine conversion in Christ will enable us to change the way we think and act.

First, we must regain humility and recognize the limits of our powers, and most importantly, the limits of our knowledge and judgment. We have been making decisions, taking actions, and assigning values that are leading us away from the world as it should be, away from the design of God for creation, away from all that is essential for a healthy planet and a healthy commonwealth of people. A new approach and a new culture are needed, based on the centrality of the human person within creation and inspired by environmentally ethical behavior stemming from our triple relationship to God, to self, and to creation. Such an ethics fosters interdependence and stresses the principles of universal solidarity, social justice, and responsibility, in order to promote a true culture of life.

Secondly, we must frankly admit that humankind is entitled to something better than what we see around us.

We and, much more, our children and future generations are entitled to a better world, a world free from degradation, violence and bloodshed, a world of generosity and love.

Thirdly, aware of the value of prayer, we must implore God the Creator to enlighten people everywhere regarding the duty to respect and carefully guard creation.

We therefore invite all men and women of good will to ponder the importance of the following ethical goals:

1. To think of the world's children when we reflect on and evaluate our options for action.

2. To be open to study the true values based on the natural law that sustain every human culture.

3. To use science and technology in a full and constructive way, while recognizing that the findings of science have always to be evaluated in the light of the centrality of the human person, of the common good, and of the inner purpose of creation. Science may help us to correct the mistakes of the past, in order to enhance the spiritual and material well-being of the present and future generations. It is love for our children that will show us the path that we must follow into the future.

4. To be humble regarding the idea of ownership and to be open to the demands of solidarity. Our mortality and our weakness of judgment together warn us not to take irreversible actions with what we choose to regard as our property during our brief stay on this earth. We have not been entrusted with unlimited power over creation, we are only stewards of the common heritage.

5. To acknowledge the diversity of situations and responsibilities in the work for a better world environment. We do not expect every person and every institution to assume the same burden. Everyone has a part to play, but for the demands of justice and charity to be respected the most affluent societies must carry the greater burden, and from them is demanded a sacrifice greater than can be offered by the poor. Religions, governments, and institutions are faced by many different situations; but on the basis of the principle of subsidiarity all of them can take on some tasks, some part of the shared effort.

6. To promote a peaceful approach to disagreement about how to live on this earth, about how to share it and use it, about what to change and what to leave unchanged. It is not our desire to evade controversy about the environment, for we trust in the capacity of human reason and the path of dialogue to reach agreement. We commit ourselves to respect the views of all who disagree with us, seeking solutions through open exchange, without resorting to oppression and domination.

It is not too late. God's world has incredible healing powers. Within a single generation, we could steer the earth toward our children's future.

Let that generation start now, with God's help and blessing.

Rome—Venice
June 10, 2002

NOTES

1. See the telling of this story in Brian Swimme and Thomas Berry, *The Universe Story*.

2. Although we use the phrase "the environmental crisis" in its singular form we recognize that our current circumstances cannot be described as a singular event, but rather as a series of events with multiple causes and consequences. Moreover, in recognizing the complex plural nature of our environmental crises, we also acknowledge that its scale and impact are now evident around the globe. See documentation of this in *The State of the World* reports for the last two decades from the Worldwatch Institute in Washington, D.C. See also the *Millennium Assessment Report* of the World Resources Institute. One of the first persons to recognize the critical nature of the environmental crisis was Fairborn Osborn in his book *Our Plundered Planet* (Boston: Little Brown, 1948).

3. We are using the term evolution to include both the universe and the earth although we recognize the fact that some scientists prefer to us it only to refer to the Earth. Eric Chaisson refers to Cosmic Evolution in his book of the same name, *Cosmic Evolution: The Rise of Complexity in Nature* (Cambridge, MA.: Harvard University Press, 2001).

4. See the website on the sixth extinction created by David Ulansey: www.well.com/user/davidu/extinction.html. See also Niles Eldredge, *Life in the Balance: Humanity and the Biodiversity Crisis* (Princeton, NJ: Princeton University Press, 1998). Eldredge was a primary curator for the Hall of Biodiversity.

5. While it is true that the vast majority of species that existed in the past have gone extinct in earlier periods due to meteor collisions, climate change and other factors, the realization that humans are now causing this sixth extinction spasm marks the present period as unique. There are multiple modes of human

intervention in natural processes, namely, destruction of habitat, use of resources, deleterious technologies, pollution of ecosystems, and population explosion. By becoming a planetary presence we are now threatening the life and future of other species. It is also important to note that clearly within nature predator/ prey interaction is widespread. This has been the case in evolutionary biology where species have their niches and limitations. However, because of our expansion as a planetary species, we will now determine, to a certain, which species may survive this particular extinction period and which will not. It is a responsibility of life-transforming proportions. For example, whether the great apes, our closest mammal relation, will go extinct is a major question and a primary concern of the Great Apes Project.

6. See E.O. Wilson's article "Is Humanity Suicidal?" in the *New York Times Sunday Magazine* (May 30th, 1993) and Peter Ravens's Presidential Address to the American Association for the Advancement of Science in Boston in February 2002.

7. Within the Christian tradition, the Creationist movement denies the validity of the scientific story of evolution. While religious anti-evolutionism has received significant notice in the United States, it is a minority position within the world's religions, although it has some counterparts in Judaism and Islam. Many of the other world religions do not share this view, since they do not begin with a doctrine of Creation. This is true, for example, of the Asian traditions of Buddhism, Confucianism, and Daoism.

8. One of the early voices speaking to the importance of a religious response to the environment is John Cobb, *Is it Too Late?* (First published by Bruce in 1972 and then reissued in 1995 by Environmental Ethics Books.)

9. As Joanna Macy has suggested they are entering their Gaian phase.

10. The critique of Christianity in relation to the environmental crisis first arose with Lynn White's article "The Historical Roots of Our Ecologic Crisis" in *Science* 155 (10th March, 1967). Many theologians have responded eloquently to the challenge of the environmental crisis, for example, John Cobb, Matthew Fox, John Haught, Dieter Hessel, Elizabeth Johnson, Gordon Kaufman, Catherine Keller, Jay McDaniel, Sallie McFague, Daniel Maguire, James Nash, Larry Rasmussen, Rosemary Ruether,

Paul Santmire, Joseph Sittler, and Loren Wilkinson. See Dieter Hessel and Rosemary Ruether, eds., *Christianty and Ecology* (Cambridge, MA.: Harvard Center for the Study of World Religions, 2000).

11. Thomas Berry, *Dream of the Earth* (San Francisco: Sierra Club Books, 1988).

12. I am indebted to Yi Fu Tuan for the phrase "hearth and cosmos." See his book *Cosmos and Hearth: A Cosmopolite's Viewpoint* (Minneapolis: University of Minnesota Press, 1996).

13. The term "Axial Age" was first used by the German philosopher Karl Jaspers. See his *The Origin and Goal of History* (London: Routledge, 1953).

14. An example is the series of monographs from SUNY Press edited by David Ray Griffin on Constructive Postmodern Thought. See also a rigorous analysis of the limits of progress and economic development models in Richard Norgaard, *Development Betrayed* (New York: Routledge, 1994).

15. We are using the term "religion and ecology" rather than "religion and environment" to indicate the deeply interconnected dimensions of the natural world, with humans embedded within, not apart from, nature. The term "environment" can connote a distance from nature as something objective and distinct from humans.

16. See for example the work of John Cobb, *The Earthist Challenge to Economism: A Theological Critique of the World Bank* (New York: St. Martin's Press, 1999) and Sallie McFague, *Life Abundant: Rethinking Theology and Economy for a Planet in Peril* (Minneapolis: Fortress Press, 2001).

17. For some forty years, the Institute for Religion in an Age of Science (IRAS) based in Chicago has held conferences and published the journal *Zygon*. For the last twenty years, the Center for Theology and the Natural Sciences (CTNS) based in Berkeley has held conferences and workshops, supported new courses, and published books in this area.

18. In addition, the traditional world religions need to be sensitive to wisdom coming from indigenous religions or from the so-called nature religions and secular environmental ethics that have inspired various environmental movements.

19. The books published from the Center for the Study of World Religions and Harvard University Press include Mary Evelyn Tucker and Duncan Williams, eds., *Buddhism and Ecology* (1997); Mary Evelyn Tucker and John Berthrong, eds., *Confucianism and Ecology* (1998); Dieter Hessel and Rosemary Radford Ruether, eds., *Christianity and Ecology* (2000); Christopher Key Chapple and Mary Evelyn Tucker, eds., *Hinduism and Ecology* (2000); John Grim, ed., *Indigenous Traditions and Ecology* (2000); N.J. Girardot, James Miller, and Liu Xiaogan, eds., *Daoism and Ecology* (2001); Christopher Key Chapple, ed., *Jainism and Ecology* (2002); Hava Tirosh Samuelson, ed., *Judaism and Ecology* (2002); Rosemary Bernard, ed., *Shinto and Ecology* (2003); Azim Nanji, Frederick Denny, and Azizan Baharuddin, eds., *Islam and Ecology* (2003).

20. The term "more than human" has been used by David Abram in his book *The Spell of the Sensuous: Perception and Language in a More-than-Human World* (New York: Pantheon, 1996).

21. With this is mind, Mary Evelyn Tucker and John Grim edited a special issue of the journal *Daedalus* that brought together scholars of the world religions with scientists, policy makers, and educators around the issue of global warming: "Religion and Ecology: Can the Climate Change?" *Daedalus* (Fall 2001). The issue is available on the internet at www.amacad.org/publications/daedalus.htm.

22. See www.earthdialogues.org.

23. This was especially the prediction of the sociologist of religion Peter Berger and others. See *Sacred Canopy* (Garden City: Doubleday, 1967).

24. See the Orbis Book Series on "Faith Meets Faith," edited by Paul Knitter. See also Leonardo Boff, *Ecology and Liberation: A New Paradigm* (Maryknoll: Orbis, 1995).

25. See www.earthcharter.org.

26. See William Theodore de Bary and Tu Weiming, eds., *Confucianism and Human Rights* (New York: Columbia University Press, 1997).

27. For use of the term "multidisciplinary" in contrast to "interdisciplinary" see George Rupp, "Religion, Modern Secular Culture, and Ecology," in Mary Evelyn Tucker and John Grim, ed.,

NOTES

"Religion and Ecology: Can the Climate Change?" *Daedalus* (Fall 2001), p. 27.

28. Many secular environmental movements and institutions have strong ethical motivations behind their activities and these are seen as separate from religious motivations. It is also true, however, that religious-like motivations are present in many secular environmental movements. See a discussion of this in Bronislaw Szerzynski, "The Varieties of Ecological Piety" in *Worldviews: Environment, Culture, Religion* Volume 1, No. 1 (April 1997), pp. 37–55.

29. See Mircea Eliade, *The Sacred and Profane* (New York: Harper, 1953).

30. These are all documented in chapters in the individual volumes in the Harvard book series on Religions of the World and Ecology. See note 19 above. Important work on ecological rituals is being done by deep ecologists such as Joanna Macy and John Seed. See especially the description of the Council of All Beings in John Seed, Joanna Macy, Pat Fleming, and Arne Naess, *Thinking Like A Mountain* (Philadelphia: New Society, 1988).

31. See for example, Rosemary Ruether, ed., *Women Healing the Earth: Third World Women on Ecology, Feminism, and Religion* (Maryknoll: Orbis, 1996).

32. The movement, which began in Britain, has had demonstrable influence in decisions to forgive debts in more than twenty countries. See www.jubilee.2000uk.org.

33. See the Orbis series on "Ecology and Justice" edited by Mary Evelyn Tucker and John Grim.

34. For statements on the environment from various religious groups see the Forum on Religion and Ecology website: http//:environment.harvard.edu/religion.

35. See for example Paul Santmire, *The Travail of Nature: The Ambiguous Ecological Promise of Christian Theology* (Minneapolis: Fortress, 1985).

36. The idea of detachment from the fruits of one's actions (*karma phalla*) is in the *Bhagavad Gita* (Chapter 5, verse 12).

37. See for example, Dennis Edwards, *Jesus and the Cosmos* (Mahwah, NJ: Paulist Press, 1991) and Ewert Cousins, *The Cosmic Christ of the Twenty-first Century*.

38. Matthew Fox, *Original Blessing* (Santa Fe: Bear and Company, 1983) and *The Coming of the Cosmic Christ* (San Francisco: Harper and Row, 1988).

39. The word "anthropocosmic" is used by Tu Weiming in *Confucian Thought: Selfhood as Creative Transformation* (Albany: State University of New York Press, 1985).

40. Tu Weiming, "Neo-Confucian Religiosity and Human-Relatedness," in his *Confucian Thought: Selfhood as Creative Transformation* (Albany: State University of New York Press, 1985), p. 132.

41. William Theodore de Bary and Irene Bloom, eds., *Sources of Chinese Tradition* (New York: Columbia University Press, 1999), pp. 682–83.

42. Rachel Carson, *The Sense of Wonder* (New York: Harper and Row, 1956). Similarly Morris Berman called for *The Reenchantment of the World* (New York: Bantam, 1984).

43. Melvin Konner, *The Tangled Wing: Biological Constraints on the Human Spirit* (New York: Holt, 1982), p. 488. Konner continues: "It must be reinstated in relation not only to the natural world but to the human world as well. We must once again experience the human soul as soul, and not just as a buzz of bioelectricity; the human will as will, not just a surge of hormones; the human heart not as a fibrous, sticky pump, but as the metaphoric organ of understanding. We need not believe in them as metaphysical entities—they are as real as the flesh and blood they are made of. But we must believe in them as entities; not as analyzed fragments but as wholes made real by our contemplation of them, by the words we use to talk of them, by the way we have transmuted them to speech. We must stand in awe of them as unassailable, even though they are dissected before our eyes.

"As for the natural world, we must restore wonder there, too. We could start with that photograph of the Earth. It may be our last chance. Even now it is being used in geography lessons, taken for granted by small children. We were the first generation to have seen it, the last generation not to take it for granted. Will we remember what it meant to us? How fine the Earth looked, dangled in space? How pretty against the endless black? How round? How very breakable? How small? It is up to us to try and experience a sense of wonder about it that will save it before it is too late. If we cannot, we may do the final damage in our lifetimes. If we can, we may change the course of history and, consequently, the course of evolution, setting the human lineage on a path toward a new evolutionary plateau."

44. Rudolph Otto, *The Idea of the Holy*, translated by John Harvey (London: Oxford University Press, 1926).

45. See John Cobb, *Sustainability: Economics, Ecology, and Justice* (Maryknoll: Orbis, 1992), for a collection of Cobb's writings on the subject.

BASIC BIBLIOGRAPHY
ON RELIGION AND ECOLOGY

Barnhill, David Landis, and Roger S. Gottlieb, eds. 2001. *Deep Ecology and World Religions: New Essays on Sacred Ground*. Albany: State University of New York Press.

Batchelor, Martine, and Kerry Brown, eds. 1992. *Buddhism and Ecology*. London: Cassell and World Wide Fund for Nature.

Berry, Thomas. 1988. *The Dream of the Earth*. San Francisco: Sierra Club Books.

————. 1999. *The Great Work*. New York: Bell Tower.

Boff, Leonardo. 1995. *Ecology and Liberation: A New Paradigm*. Maryknoll: Orbis.

Cadman, David, and John Carey, eds. 2002. *A Sacred Trust: Ecology and Spiritual Vision*. London: Temenos Academy and the Prince's Foundation.

Callicott, J. Baird. 1997. *Earth's Insights: A Multicultural Survey of Ecological Ethics from the Mediterranean Basin to the Australian Outback*. Berkeley: University of California Press.

Callicott, J. Baird, and Roger T. Ames, eds. 1989. *Nature in Asian Traditions of Thought*. Albany: State University of New York Press.

Chapple, Christopher Key, ed. 2002. *Jainism and Ecology: Nonviolence in the Web of Life*. Cambridge, MA: Harvard Center for the Study of World Religions and Harvard University Press.

Chapple, Christopher Key, and Mary Evelyn Tucker, eds. 2000. *Hinduism and Ecology: The Intersection of Earth, Sky, and Water*. Cambridge, MA: Harvard Center for the Study of World Religions and Harvard University Press.

Chryssavgis, John, ed. 2003. *Cosmic Grace, Humble Prayer: Ecological Vision of the Green Patriarch Bartholemew*. Grand Rapids: Eerdmans.

Cobb, John B., Jr. 1995 [1972]. *Is It Too Late? A Theology of Ecology*. Denton, TX: Environmental Ethics Books.

Daneel, Marthinus. 2001. *African Earthkeepers: Wholistic Interfaith Mission*. Maryknoll: Orbis.

Devall, Bill and George Sessions. 1985. *Deep Ecology: Living As if Nature Mattered*, Salt Lake City: Peregrine Smith.

Foltz, Richard, ed. 2002. *Worldviews, Religion, and the Environment: A Global Anthology*. Belmont: Wadsworth.

Fox, Matthew. 1988. *The Coming of the Cosmic Christ: The Healing of Mother Earth and the Birth of a Global Renaissance*. San Francisco: Harper.

Gardner, Gary, ed. 2002. *Invoking the Spirit: Religion and Spirituality in the Quest for a Sustainable World*. Worldwatch Paper 164. Washington, DC: Worldwatch Institute.

Gebara, Ivone. 1999. *Longing for Running Water: Ecofeminism and Liberation*. Minneapolis: Augsburg Fortress.

Girardot, N.J., James Miller, and Liu Xiaogan, eds. 2001. *Daoism and Ecology: Ways within a Cosmic Landscape*. Cambridge, MA: Harvard Center for the Study of World Religions and Harvard University Press.

Gottlieb, Roger, ed. 1995. *This Sacred Earth: Religion, Nature, Environment*. New York: Routledge.

Grim, John A. 1983. *The Shaman: Patterns of Siberian and Ojibway Healing*. Norman: University of Oklahoma Press.

———, ed. 2001. *Indigenous Traditions and Ecology: The Interbeing of Cosmology and Community*. Cambridge, MA: Harvard Center for the Study of World Religions and Harvard University Press.

Tirosh-Samuelson, Hava, ed. 2002. *Judaism and Ecology: Created World and Revealed World*. Cambridge, MA: Harvard Center for the Study of World Religions and Harvard University Press.

Hargrove, Eugene C., ed. 1986. *Religion and Environmental Crisis*. Athens, GA: University of Georgia Press.

Hessel, Dieter, and Rosemary Radford Ruether, eds. 2000. *Christianity and Ecology: Seeking the Well-Being of Earth and Humans*. Cambridge, MA: Center for the Study of World Religions and Harvard University Press.

Hull, Fritz, ed. 1993. *Earth and Spirit: The Spiritual Dimension of the Environmental Crisis*. New York: Continuum.

Izzi Dien, Mawil Y. 2000. *The Environmental Dimensions of Islam*. Cambridge: Lutterworth.

Kaza, Stephanie and Kenneth Kraft, eds. 2000. *Dharma Rain: Sources of Buddhist Environmentalism*. Boston: Shambhala.

Kellert, Stephen R., and Timothy J. Farnham, eds. 2002. *The Good in Nature and Humanity: Connecting Science and Spirituality with the Natural World*. Washington, DC: Island Press.

Kinsley, David. 1995. *Ecology and Religion: Ecological Spirituality in Cross-Cultural Perspective*. Englewood Cliffs: Prentice-Hall.

Knitter, Paul F. 1995. *One Earth, Many Religions: Multifaith Dialogue and Global Responsibility*. Maryknoll: Orbis.

Mander, Jerry. 1991. *In the Absence of the Sacred: The Failure of Technology and the Survival of the Indian Nations*. San Francisco: Sierra Club.

Matthews, Clifford N., Mary Evelyn Tucker, and Philip Hefner, eds. 2001. *When Worlds Converge: What Science and Religion Tell Us about the Story of the Universe and Our Place in It*. Chicago: Open Court.

McDaniel, Jay B. 1989. *Of God and Pelicans: A Theology of Reverence for Life*. Louisville: Westminster/John Knox Press.

McDonagh, Sean. 1990. *The Greening of the Church*. Maryknoll: Orbis.

McFague, Sallie. 1987. *Models of God: Theology for an Ecological, Nuclear Age*. Philadelphia: Fortress.

McGrath, Alister E. 2002. *The Reenchantment of Nature: The Denial of Religion and the Ecological Crisis*. New York: Doubleday.

Nasr, Seyyed Hossein. 1996. *Religion and the Order of Nature*. New York: Oxford University Press.

Nelson, Lance E., ed. 1998. *Purifying the Earthly Body of God*. Albany: State University of New York Press.

Rasmussen, Larry. 1996. *Earth Community, Earth Ethics*. Maryknoll: Orbis.

Ruether, Rosemary Radford. 1992. *Gaia and God*. San Francisco: Harper.

Ruether, Rosemary Radford, and Dieter Hessel, eds. 2000. *Christianity and Ecology: Seeking the Well-Being of Earth and Humans*. Cambridge, MA: Harvard University Press.

Santmire, Paul. 1985. *The Travail of Nature: The Ambiguous Ecological Promise of Christian Theology*. Philadelphia : Fortress.

Spretnak, Charlene. 1991. *States of Grace: The Recovery of Meaning in the Post-modern Age*. San Francisco: Harper.

Spring, David, and Eileen Spring, eds. 1974. *Ecology and Religion in History*. New York: Harper Collins.

Suzuki, David, and Peter Knudtson. 1992. *Wisdom of the Elders: Sacred Native Stories of Nature*. New York: Bantam.

Swimme, Brian, and Thomas Berry. 1992. *The Universe Story*. San Francisco: Harper.

Tanner, Ralph, and Colin Mitchell. 2002. *Religion and the Environment*. New York" Palgrave.

Toolan, David 2001. At Home in the Cosmos. Maryknoll: Orbis.

Tucker, Mary Evelyn, and John Berthrong, eds. 1998. *Confucianism and Ecology: The Interrelation of Heaven, Earth and Humans*. Cambridge, MA: Harvard Center for the Study of World Religions and Harvard University Press.

Tucker, Mary Evelyn, and John A. Grim. 1994. *Worldviews and Ecology: Religion, Philosophy, and the Environment*. Maryknoll: Orbis (Fifth edition 2002).

————, eds. 2001. Religion and Ecology: Can the Climate Change? *Daedalus* (Fall 2001).

Tucker, Mary Evelyn, and Duncan Williams, eds. 1997. *Buddhism and Ecology: The Interconnection of Dharma and Deeds*. Cambridge, MA: Harvard Center for the Study of World Religions and Harvard University Press.

Waskow, Arthur, ed. 2000. *Torah of the Earth*. Two volumes. Woodstock, VT: Jewish Lights.

THE INSTITUTE
FOR WORLD RELIGIONS

With the understanding that spiritual values are
central to the human experience, the Institute for
World Religions exists to advance mutual understanding among the world's spiritual traditions. The
Institute for World Religions facilitates shared inquiry
into the founding visions of the world's faiths so that
all might learn from the others' strengths while
preserving the integrity of their own.

The Institute for World Religions is also committed
to providing an open forum where clergy, theologians,
philosophers, scientists, educators, and individuals
from a wide variety of disciplines can examine the
role of religion in a modern world. All of the Institute's
activities take place in an atmosphere of mutual
respect and promote the universal human capacity for
goodness and wisdom.

Established in 1976, the Institute was the direct
result of the inspiration and planning of the Buddhist

Chan Patriarch Hsüan Hua and Roman Catholic Cardinal Yu-Bin. Both of these distinguished international leaders in religion and education believed that harmony among the world's religions is an indispensable prerequisite for a just and peaceful world. Each shared the conviction that every religion should affirm humanity's common bonds and rise above narrow sectarian differences.

In keeping with its mission, the Institute offers programs designed to bring the major religious traditions together in discourse with each other and with the contemporary world. Its proximity to the University of California at Berkeley, Stanford University, the Graduate Theological Union, and the rich academic, religious, and cultural environment of the San Francisco Bay area provides an ideal environment for the Institute's programs.

INDEX